NEW DIRECTIONS FOR ADULT AND CONTINUING EDUCATION

Susan Imel, *Ohio State University*
COEDITOR-IN-CHIEF

Jovita M. Ross-Gordon, *Southwest Texas State University*
COEDITOR-IN-CHIEF

New Perspectives on Designing and Implementing Professional Development of Teachers of Adults

Kathleen P. King
Fordham University

Patricia A. Lawler
Widener University

EDITORS

Number 98, Summer 2003

JOSSEY-BASS
San Francisco

NEW PERSPECTIVES ON DESIGNING AND IMPLEMENTING PROFESSIONAL
DEVELOPMENT OF TEACHERS OF ADULTS
Kathleen P. King, Patricia A. Lawler (eds.)
New Directions for Adult and Continuing Education, no. 98
Susan Imel, Jovita M. Ross-Gordon, Coeditors-in-Chief

Microfilm copies of issues and articles are available in 16mm and 35mm,
as well as microfiche in 105mm, through University Microfilms Inc., 300
North Zeeb Road, Ann Arbor, Michigan 48106-1346.

ISSN 1052-2891   electronic ISSN 1536-0717

NEW DIRECTIONS FOR ADULT AND CONTINUING EDUCATION is part of The
Jossey-Bass Higher and Adult Education Series and is published quarterly
by Wiley Subscription Services, Inc., A Wiley company, at Jossey-Bass,
989 Market Street, San Francisco, California 94103-1741. Periodicals
postage paid at San Francisco, California, and at additional mailing offices.
Postmaster: Send address changes to New Directions for Adult and Continuing Education, Jossey-Bass, 989 Market Street, San Francisco, California, 94103-1741.

SUBSCRIPTIONS cost $70.00 for individuals and $149.00 for institutions,
agencies, and libraries.

EDITORIAL CORRESPONDENCE should be sent to the Editor-in-Chief, Susan
Imel, ERIC/ACVE, 1900 Kenny Road, Columbus, Ohio 43210-1090.
e-mail: imel.l@osu.edu.

Cover photograph by Wernher Krutein/PHOTOVAULT © 1990.

www.josseybass.com

Contents

EDITORS' NOTES

Today's teachers of adults are facing challenges that affect their organizations and professional roles as never before: technology, diverse learner populations, demands for accountability and productivity, and the increased consumerism of the participants. Professional development activities are one of the strategies used to meet these challenges, yet these initiatives are often greeted with a less than enthusiastic response because their value and usefulness to practice are not always recognized. Discovering how to change that perception—and how to create and provide effective and successful professional development—is crucial today.

Along with others, we believe that educators themselves need to be viewed as adult learners and that professional development needs to be grounded in the principles and practices of adult learning and adult education (Cranton, 1996; Lawler and King, 2000). Whether teachers of adults are working in higher education, adult literacy, or corporate training, there has been little evidence that administrators and professional developers view these teachers from an adult learning perspective.

The first part of this volume provides the conceptual background for this perspective on teachers of adults as adult learners. Chapter One presents the current trends and issues surrounding the professional development of teachers of adults. King and Lawler take the perspective that teachers of adults are themselves adult learners. Furthermore, although diverse in their settings, backgrounds, and learning needs, they face many of the same challenges today because their work is constantly changing. All of these factors frame the volume's discussion of professional development as adult learning.

Chapter Two, by Lawler, describes in detail the perspective of teachers of adults as adult learners in their professional development and their teaching and learning experiences. The Adult Learning Model for Faculty Development (Lawler and King, 2000) is used to provide a framework for discussing the volume's vision of professional development. This chapter reviews the adult learning principles that are the basis of this model. By becoming familiar with this model, professional developers can provide professional development activities from a perspective that conceptualizes and addresses educators of adults with their needs and potential as adult learners. Such a perspective can provide a challenging and rewarding experience for all involved.

In Chapter Three, Daley discusses learner-centered teaching and learning and how they can be applied to educators' development. Drawing on her own experience as a participant in different kinds of professional development, she provides a cogent discussion of the benefits of the learner-centered model. Her review of the learning and teaching orientations literature has special meaning for the professional development of educators of adults. Recognizing that reflective practice is a key component of meaningful professional development, she also presents three strategies to guide educators as they contemplate their own professional development and to assist developers in guiding teachers of adults to do so.

In Chapter Four, Cranton and King discuss transformative learning as a professional development goal. In recognition that more than skills attainment and increased test scores should be the intent of professional development, this chapter explores how it can instead lead to the development of authentic, individuated, and critically reflective practitioners. Five specific strategies are described: action plans, reflective activities, case studies, curriculum development, and critical theory discussions. Building on the grounding literature of transformational learning, Cranton and King present a compelling image of how professional development can lead to deep, significant personal and professional learning opportunities and change among educators of adults when it is designed with this purpose in mind.

The second part of the book moves toward application, addressing two important concerns in professional development: motivation and new technology learning. In Chapter Five Wlodkowski discusses the ever-present issue of motivating teachers and trainers for professional development. He proposes and develops the Motivational Framework for Culturally Responsive Teaching Model as a guide to facilitate participation, learning, and transfer of learning through professional development. In an age of increasingly multicultural environments, Wlodkowski provides insight into how to validate diversity and build a welcoming and motivational environment for professional development. His recommendations include establishing inclusion, developing attitude, enhancing meaning, and engendering competence.

In Chapter Six, King demonstrates how the ubiquitous challenge of rapidly changing technology provides a key context for professional development that can meet the needs of educators of adults. King presents an understanding of faculty need and risks while also providing specific strategies and approaches to use in teaching and learning educational technology. Often educational technology professional development focuses on skills acquisition and troubleshooting; King instead approaches such learning opportunities as the possible basis for what she calls journeys of transformation (King, 2003). Understanding the many personal, social, and professional conditions and risks that underlie technology learning for teachers of adults presents a new view of educational technology professional development. This chapter describes several principles and strategies to cultivate professional development in educational technology that may lead to transformation.

Finally, the third part of the book discusses the specific contexts of adult education and the needs of educators of adults in each of them. Experts from the areas of higher education, adult basic education, and corporate training portray the needs of their educators and make recommendations for practice. Brancato in Chapter Seven describes the needs of faculty in higher education and the challenges they face in their classrooms and development. She suggests that looking at higher education faculty as learners in a learning organization can provide a more successful experience for those educators and ultimately for their students. This learning organization framework leads to recommendations for how to employ Senge's (1990) five components in professional development.

In Chapter Eight, Georges Marceau, a regional director of a staff consortium of adult basic education, presents an overview of what is happening in the United States with regard to the needs of these educators in their diverse classrooms. He also looks at the forms that professional development of adult educators take in different geographic regions and synthesizes recommendations for practice.

In Chapter Nine, Meyer and Marsick present the needs and context of corporate trainers. By way of four examples and a review of the literature, the authors explain which skills and abilities should be elements of the professional development of trainers. Their recommendations for practice cover design and delivery, multiple perspectives, a variety of delivery systems and locations, and transfer of learning to the workplace.

Chapter Ten concludes the volume with a synthesis of the proposed changes, challenges, and future directions for the professional development of teachers of adults that have been presented. After reviewing the vision of the book, Lawler and King also suggest two new directions for the advancement of the field.

By bringing together this understanding with strategies to motivate, equip, and support teachers as adult learners, this volume will be a valuable resource as a starting point for teacher renewal. In addition, the sourcebook also provides examples of how such a vision and design of professional development can be applied in higher education, adult basic education, and corporate training. This volume facilitates the introduction, discussion, and application of this vision for assisting educators of adults in their pursuit of lifelong learning and professional excellence.

This volume is truly a collaborative work, with experts in areas of adult learning, faculty development, human resource development, and adult education all focusing on the needs of professional development of teachers of adults. We hope that bringing together the insights from the many perspectives represented provides a new lens from which to view the needs of educators of adults and to plan and deliver development that will encourage them in their professional growth.

Kathleen P. King
Patricia A. Lawler
Editors

References

Cranton, P. A. *Professional Development as Transformative Learning*. San Francisco: Jossey-Bass, 1996.

King, K. P. *Keeping Pace with Technology: Educational Technology That Transforms*. Vol. 2: *The Challenge and Promise for Higher Education Faculty*. Cresskill, N.J.: Hampton Press, 2003.

Lawler, P. A., and King, K. P. *Planning for Effective Faculty Development: Using Adult Learning Strategies*. Malabar, Fla.: Krieger, 2000.

Senge, P. *The Fifth Discipline: The Art and Practice of the Learning Organization*. New York: Doubleday, 1990.

KATHLEEN P. KING *is an associate professor and program director of adult education and human resource development at Fordham University's Graduate School of Education in New York City.*

PATRICIA A. LAWLER *is a professor in the Center for Education, Widener University, Chester, Pennsylvania.*

1

This chapter introduces the distinct perspective that this sourcebook brings to the literature and practice of professional development while placing it in the context of current trends and issues in the field.

Trends and Issues in the Professional Development of Teachers of Adults

Kathleen P. King, Patricia A. Lawler

Carol has just sent out the flyer on campuswide faculty development programs. She hopes she has struck a good balance between sessions focusing on improving active learning in the traditional classroom and sessions on how to facilitate Web-based classes. Sara and Juan struggle to find topics and formats for the professional development of their adult learning center's ESL and literacy teachers that will be relevant to their classrooms and provide a basis for sustained growth in their professional lives. In the state-of-the-art corporate classroom, Lee faces a roomful of trainers who have recently been downsized, and at age twenty-eight, he wonders what his credibility will be with these fifty year olds.

What do all of these professional developers have in common? How are their tasks and challenges similar? Each is concerned with educating educators of adults. Although the settings are diverse, the problems and concerns these developers face are similar.

A New Vision: Unity in Diverse Settings

Today, teachers of adults face a growing need to teach their learners efficiently and quickly while ensuring successful outcomes. How can our professional developers Carol, Sara, Juan, and Lee prepare their educators to meet these challenges? The natural place to provide ongoing support in gaining needed learning, skills, and support for educators is professional development. However, while many professional developers come from an education and training background, few are schooled in adult learning. Our perspective provides for designing and implementing professional

NEW DIRECTIONS FOR ADULT AND CONTINUING EDUCATION, no. 98, Summer 2003 © Wiley Periodicals, Inc.

development for teachers of adults with a focus on understanding adult learning, the different contexts in which teachers of adults work, and the distinctive needs of each group of them.

Depending on what kind of teacher of adults one was, historically one generally had different options for professional development: if you were a college teacher, professional development centered on your discipline, not on whom you taught; if you were in adult basic education, it focused on content, regulations, and testing; and if you were in the training and development sector, it focused on teaching for increased productivity and profit. Yet teachers of adults are themselves adult learners whose learning differences and needs for application, critical reflection, respect, and support need to be understood. While recognizing that each context for teachers of adults has different expectations, needs, and limitations, a broader vision of professional development highlights the similarities among the challenges.

New demands are making us look at professional development in different ways. In this age of accountability, neither teachers of adults nor professional developers are exempt. We need to assess and determine the impact of the many changes dominating our daily lives. A proactive approach enables the professional developer to be a leader in preparing to meet new challenges. This new view of professional development provides a framework through which to design, plan, and deliver professional development that sustains sound pedagogy and andragogy and incorporates new needs.

The concern of this text is the professional development of educators and how we can better understand and address their needs and challenges. Among the influences on teachers of adults are their perspective, practice, and individual professional and learning needs. In addition, institutional needs create a "current context" in which they must succeed. Finally, educators confront many trends and issues in these settings that affect their needs for professional development. Figure 1.1 provides an overview of the place of professional development for teachers of adults in the scope of organizations and institutions. We turn first to the climate and current context in which these teachers work.

Current Context for Professional Development

The climate for the professional development of teachers of adults is far from monolithic. Rather, professional developers are under pressure from many constituencies in varying conditions. In today's organizational climate professional developers must deal successfully with students, academic concerns, finances, and current trends and issues.

In the past, student performance was one focus. Whether students must pass the GED or a licensing exam or increase their productivity in the workplace, the standard has been clear and the educator's responsibility heavy. But today, shifts in the adult student population affect this quantitative

Figure 1.1. Professional Development Dynamics

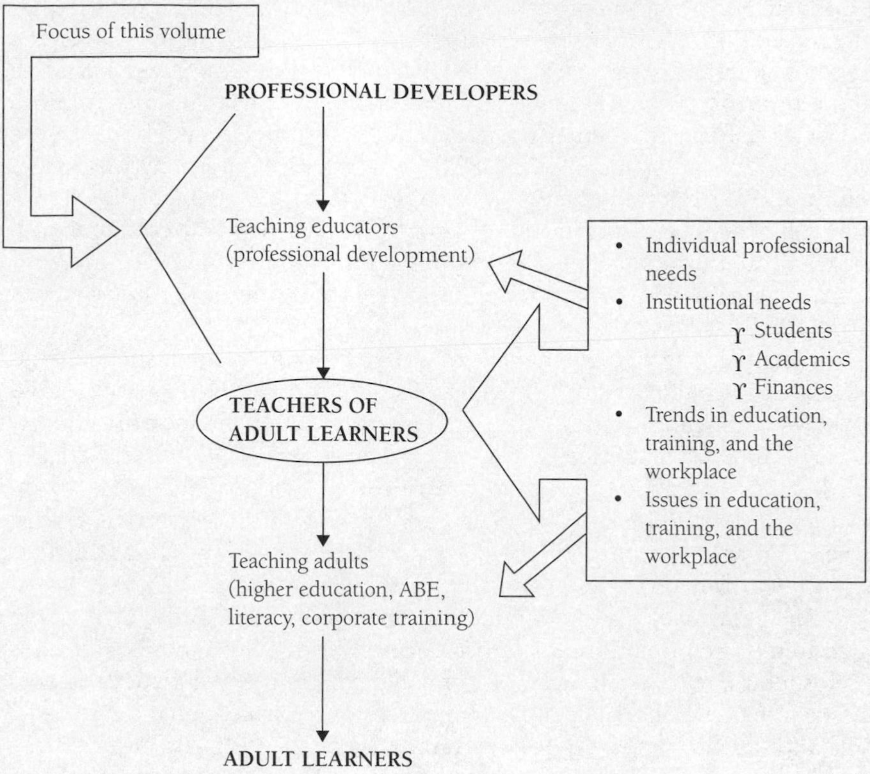

Focus of this volume

PROFESSIONAL DEVELOPERS

Teaching educators
(professional development)

- Individual professional
  needs
- Institutional needs
  - ϒ Students
  - ϒ Academics
  - ϒ Finances
- Trends in education,
  training, and the
  workplace
- Issues in education,
  training, and the
  workplace

TEACHERS OF
ADULT LEARNERS

Teaching adults
(higher education, ABE,
literacy, corporate training)

ADULT LEARNERS

emphasis on achievement. As the general and working population has become increasingly diverse in recent years, educators face the varied needs of students of different nationalities, languages, gender, sexual orientation, and educational preparation (Merriam and Caffarella, 1999). No longer are some vocations the closed fraternity of white middle-class men; instead, both women and men are working in most jobs, although inequities certainly still exist. How does the teacher of adults understand this changing population, meet multiple needs, and teach across multiple skill levels? These are complex demands that are essential for professional developers to understand and address.

Next there are the academic concerns. The place of testing and test preparation in educational programs is a critical area on which teachers and administrators need to agree. At a time when standardized tests are being scrutinized by both the professions and the general public, how are academic standards being determined and assessed (Schmidt, 2000)? Do development, growth, and the personal aspects of learning fit into the equation? In what ways should professional developers be prepared to assist educators in evaluating their own learning needs and determining a plan to meet them?

Financial concerns are important for any organization, whether public or private, for-profit or not-for-profit. The bottom line determines whether classes can be scheduled. As a culture of downsizing and cutbacks has become commonplace in the global marketplace, many questions arise about professional development. One of these questions that arises in times of fiscal austerity is whether professional development contributes to the organizational mission and success (Bartlett, 2002). In organizations where educators have not traditionally been concerned with enrollment (for example, in higher education), they now have to make it their concern (Brainard, 2001). If their programs or classes do not fill, or if they do not meet their learners' perceived needs, the need for and provision of their services is diminished.

Finally, the changing dynamics of our communities and businesses, and of countries around the world, affect professional development as well. Rapid changes in technology lead to more frequent training of educators in their use and application of new advances in their instruction. Privatization of workplace preparation threatens the territory of traditional higher education (Merriam and Caffarella, 1999). Distance education challenges concepts of where and when teaching and learning take place and how geographical "territory" is understood (Green and Baer, 2001; Harley, 2001).

The climate for professional development shifts constantly. Changes in technology, economic trends and forecasts, leadership models, business philosophies, political climates, cultural and community mandates, and specific contextual concerns demand the attention of professional developers. The authors of this sourcebook recognize the demanding task professional developers face in their roles as guides, leaders, mentors, and problem solvers. We therefore explore the perspective and actions of teaching educators of adults. What perspectives can provide new insights into their teaching and learning processes? Are there exemplary practices distinct to content or setting, such as adult literacy, higher education, or corporate training? Are there some principles that may be consistently applied across these fields? How can we assist professional developers and their learners in meeting the many challenges of their contexts? What holistic vision can be developed and used to improve the personal and professional growth, planning, and practice of teachers of adults?

Trends for the Future

Emerging from our current context in professional development, we envision the future of professional development as seen across the spectrum of teaching adults. As the need for education and training increases, and as our world changes around us, we are faced with several trends that will shape professional development and its impact on teachers of adults. The most significant trend, which has been with us for some time but continues to make an impact, is the *demand for the incorporation of technology into the content and delivery of professional development.* Whether they work with faculty in a community college who are interested in teaching an on-line course or they are literacy volunteers working with immigrants from Serbia, teachers of adults are faced with their own learning needs and challenges. Technology is changing the way we perceive how learning takes place and how we gather information. It is changing the speed with which we can accomplish tasks, gain knowledge, and interact with others. But technology has also created chasms and divides for those of us working with teachers of adults. Access, training, and continuing updates are critical issues in professional development, which can be strapped for funds and the latest software (Charp, 2001).

Hard on the heels of the technology trend comes the *challenge of funding for professional development.* There will continue to be inequity across the sectors of professional development. As economic cutbacks are felt across the country, increased demands for limited funds will put professional development in a precarious position. In colleges and universities, where we already see demand for accountability in the wake of spiraling tuition costs, spending funds for professional development may seem superfluous when technology and infrastructure needs go unmet. In recent years there has been a decrease in employer-based tuition funding, which has affected the educational choices of many seeking professional development at colleges, training institutions, and universities (Brownstein, 2001). States and the federal government are shifting priorities in educational funding. Although many states are demanding that teachers continue their in-service learning to stay qualified for certification, funding for educational programs and study has declined (Hebel, Schmidt, and Selingo, 2002).

As professional developers we also have been seeing a marked trend in the *diversity of adult learners and their educational settings.* Adult education in this country has grown in the last thirty years. More adults than traditional-age students are attending college today (Evelyn, 2002; U.S. Department of Education, 2002). With increased immigration, we are seeing more and more courses and programs in English for speakers of other languages (ESOL). And although the corporate world, business, and industry have been in the forefront of human resource development for most of the twentieth century, there is now renewed interest in efficiency, reengineering, and lifelong learning. Teachers of adults in a variety of settings are poised to bring about change, growth, and the development of new skills among their learners. The settings have proliferated, and the students themselves are more and more diverse in age, educational background, race and ethnicity, and economic and social status. Thus, teachers of adults are continually challenged to think beyond their own ethnocentric experiences and widen their repertoire of teaching and communication skills to meet the varied needs of their learners.

A trend specific to higher education is the *proliferation of centers for teaching and learning* (University of Kansas, 2001). With changing faculty needs, these centers are focusing on several trends in higher education. First, there is an ongoing shift from an emphasis on teaching to an emphasis on learning. Second, there is a movement from individualized professional development centering on one's discipline and research to a more student-centered, process-oriented focus on teaching and the enhancement of learning. For older and traditional faculty schooled and trained as researchers and scholars, this shift to teaching and enhancing learning may prove challenging (Alstete, 2000; Lawler and King, 2000). For those creating and conducting faculty development in campus centers, increased numbers of faculty and the diversity of faculty needs create new dilemmas.

Each of these trends has been growing stronger over the past decade. Teachers of adults are continually faced with the demands of new technologies, limited funding, a variety of educational venues, and shifts in their paradigms of teaching and learning, These trends raise issues for us to consider as we work toward a new vision for professional development.

Issues in Professional Development

As we face the future of professional development of teachers of adults, we need to recognize four other issues: *technology, professionalization, focus, and assessment.*

The proliferation of new technologies is forcing us to rethink how we use technology in our work. Whether they are drafting lesson plans, planning conferences, gathering information, or communicating with colleagues and students, teachers of adults have new ways to organize and conduct their work (King, 2003). In addition, we have to remember that teachers and trainers may be engaged in new forms of work, such as broadcasting information over e-mail to students between class sessions, holding evening office hours on-line, or developing Web pages to provide Internet-based learning resources. Professional development programs not only hold the possibility of helping teachers learn to use technology but also provide forums for them to share their questions and solutions and to discover alternatives together. Technology certainly facilitates communication, but it is also a cause for reflection and dialogue to encourage and empower educators to capture its greatest potential.

Meanwhile, the call for the professionalization of teaching has many consequences. First, we need to consider and discuss the merits and drawbacks of this movement. Second, there is the recognition of state and national associations and governing agencies to recommend or mandate uniform credentialing of teachers of adults. Third, teachers of adults need to be informed about how programs may be accredited in the future; rather than assigning responsibility for such decisions and planning to administrators alone, professional developers can provide expertise in recognizing educators' needs and interests and forums. Professional developers can play a significant role in engaging teachers of adults in fact-finding and critical examination of the meaning and consequences of such initiatives, if it is proposed and planned for them to do so. If the professionalization trend results in further need for credentialing and accreditation, it will greatly influence the future course of professional development.

Third, it is also apparent that there will be additional changes in the focus of professional development. It will likely be recognized as a conduit for providing information. However, building on our understanding of teachers of adults as lifelong learners, these expectations may be transformed to result in opportunities for critical reflection and reflective practice (Brookfield, 1995; Lawler and King, 2000). Delivering information is only the beginning of how professional development may be used as an experience of insight and growth. We also realize that educators need to be interested in current and future issues affecting their organizations. Professional development programs will be called on to raise interest and guide practice. Recognizing teachers of adults as adult learners themselves alters this deficit model perspective of corrective action to include the needs, opinions, and plans of teachers of adults. Rather than professional development meaning "training" sessions to inculcate the "party line," developers may be able to see the potential of educators and trainers exploring their worldviews and developing their voices. Teachers of adults and developers may have life-changing experiences as they grow to understand new futures, even greater passion for their profession, and a new focus.

The final issue in professional development today is assessment. Up until now little has been done to discuss and develop professional development assessment that goes beyond setting behavioral objectives, completing employee performance assessments, and monitoring "seat time." Entirely new sets of issues are raised when we begin to ask how professional development may be recognized as successful or not, what identifies successful programs, what best practices are in assessment in the multiple settings of professional development, and how comprehensive assessment can be planned for and pursued. Assessment remains a looming challenge for the field of professional development.

A New Vision for Professional Development

As these many issues and influences on professional development converge, a conceptual and active vision to guide professional developers emerges. By looking at teachers of adults as adult learners themselves, and by seeing professional development as a form of adult education, the focus shifts to the educators' individual, organizational, and personal needs. If we have a broad, integrated perspective on professional development, it goes beyond preparing educators to function well in their classrooms and leads to development of the professionals as well. This sourcebook examines four main aspects of an adult learning vision of professional development: adult education, learner-centered and transformative learning, and the pressing need

Figure 1.2. Integrative Approach to Professional Development

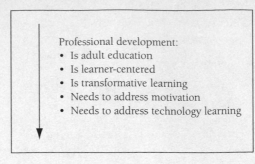

Professional development:
- Is adult education
- Is learner-centered
- Is transformative learning
- Needs to address motivation
- Needs to address technology learning

for motivation and technology learning. These markers of the organizational climate, issues, and trends will emerge time and again as we pursue the integrative approach outlined in Figure 1.2. The final chapters of this volume discuss specific contexts of professional development and detail how this vision can be applied to each. The professional development of teachers of adults has tremendous potential when looked at through the lens of adult learning.

References

Alstete, J. "Post-Tenure Faculty Development: Building a System of Faculty Improvement and Appreciation." *ASHE ERIC Higher Education Report,* 2000, 27(4).

Bartlett, T. "The Unkindest Cut: The Struggle to Save a Teaching and Learning Center." *Chronicle of Higher Education,* Mar. 22, 2002, p. A10.

Brainard, J. "University of California's President Proposes Dropping the SAT Requirement." *Chronicle of Higher Education,* Feb. 19, 2001. [http://chronicle.com/daily/2001/02/2001021901n.htm].

Brookfield, S. D. *Becoming a Critically Reflective Teacher.* San Francisco: Jossey-Bass, 1995.

Brownstein, A. "Enrollment Shifts and Last-Minute Aid Requests Signal the Onset of an Economic Downturn." *Chronicle of Higher Education,* Apr. 20, 2001, p. A14.

Charp, S. "Professional Development." *Technological Horizons in Education Journal,* June 2001. [http://www.thejournal.com/magazine/vault/A3488.cfm].

Evelyn, J. "Nontraditional Students Dominate Undergraduate Enrollments, U.S. Study Finds." *Chronicle of Higher Education,* June 4, 2002. [http://chronicle.com/daily/2002/06/2002060402n.htm].

Green, M., and Baer, M. "Global Learning in a New Age." *Chronicle of Higher Education,* Nov. 9, 2001, p. B24.

Harley, D. "Higher Education in the Digital Age: Planning for an Uncertain Future." *Syllabus Magazine,* Sept. 2001. [http://www.syllabus.com/syllabusmagazine/article.asp?id=4769].

Hebel, S., Schmidt, P., and Selingo, J. "States Face Year of Famine After a Decade of Plenty." *Chronicle of Higher Education,* Jan. 11, 2002, p. A20.

King, K. P. *Keeping Pace with Technology: Educational Technology That Transforms.* Vol. 2: *The Challenge and Promise for Higher Education Faculty.* Cresskill, N.J.: Hampton Press, 2003.

Lawler, P. A., and King, K. P. *Planning for Effective Faculty Development: Using Adult Learning Strategies.* Malabar, Fla.: Krieger, 2000.

Merriam, S., and Caffarella, R. *Learning in Adulthood.* (2nd ed.) San Francisco: Jossey-Bass, 1999.

Schmidt, P. "Faculty Outcry Greets Proposal for Competency Test at University of Texas." *Chronicle of Higher Education,* Oct. 6, 2000, p. A35.

University of Kansas Center for Teaching Excellence. *Other Teaching Centers: United States, 2001,* 2001. [http://eagle.cc.ukans.edu/~cte/resources/websites/unitedstates.html].

U.S. Department of Education. *The Condition of Education 2002.* Washington, D.C.: National Center for Education Statistics, 2002. [http://nces.ed.gov/pubs2002/2002025.pdf].

KATHLEEN P. KING is an associate professor and program director of adult education and human resource development at Fordham University's Graduate School of Education in New York City.

PATRICIA A. LAWLER is a professor in the Center for Education, Widener University, Chester, Pennsylvania.

2

As professional developers, it is imperative that we view the teacher of adults as an adult learner and the professional development activity as adult learning. This chapter presents the Adult Learning Model for Faculty Development for implementation with teachers of adults.

Teachers as Adult Learners: A New Perspective

Patricia A. Lawler

Although teachers of adults may be well-versed in working with adult learners in their particular setting, rarely do we see them reflecting on their own learning and using that reflection as a way to understand their learning needs and motivations (Brookfield, 1995). For example, an adjunct professor teaching an introduction to psychology course to returning adults at a community college may well recommend that her students keep a journal of their learning and reflect on how they learn. But she may not realize what an opportunity she herself has to reflect on her own learning by keeping a journal of her experiences in her graduate courses. Similarly, a corporate trainer who provides strategies for transfer of learning in his sessions may neglect to see how his recent conference on new technologies can be incorporated into the training programs he has to develop. These teachers of adults may also face challenges in classes, in-service, workshops, and courses that seem to turn them off instead of motivating them for growth, learning, and change. They themselves may thus find professional development irrelevant and inconsistent with their own needs.

Although we may be at ease with thinking of our various learners from an adult learning perspective, we may be shortsighted in not including teachers of adults as well. When we view teachers of adults as adult learners, and their professional development as adult education, we have at our disposal the research and literature from the fields of adult education, adult learning and development, and program development. This rich resource provides us with effective principles and practices, tried-and-true strategies, and practical applications, as well as a wealth of experience to bring to this new audience.

New Directions for Adult and Continuing Education, no. 98, Summer 2003   © Wiley Periodicals, Inc.

This chapter first focuses on this rich resource, bringing the research and literature on adult education, learning, and development into focus for those of us working with teachers of adults. Based on this foundation, the Adult Learning Model for Faculty Development will then be presented with suggestions for implementation.

Adult Learners

Adult learners share several characteristics. First, adult learners are diverse. The diversity of their life experiences, education, and personalities increases with age and shapes their outlook on educational experiences, past and present. These experiences also influence their perspective on future educational events, including their motivation to engage in professional development activities (Lawler, 1991). If our goal is to create positive professional development activities for our teachers of adults, we must remember that past experiences may not all be positive; this can influence motivation for new learning. One aspect of this is a mismatch between our teaching styles and their learning styles. An aspect of adult learner diversity is the diversity of learning styles and the various ways learners strategize to learn successfully. Many authors (Cranton, 1992; Kolb, 1984; Lawler, 1991; Merriam and Caffarella, 1999; Smith and Kolb, 1986) note the importance of understanding learning styles and encourage us to acknowledge these differences and find strategies to incorporate learning activities that are inviting and positive.

As we grow older we have more and more experiences that influence our lives and our thinking. "Adults differ from younger learners in that a younger person is still anticipating most of the responsibilities in which an adult is fully engaged. Adults are therefore more likely than younger students to personalize learning" (Taylor, Marienau, and Fiddler, 2000, p. 4). They seek to make meaning of their learning, both formal and informal, as they proceed through life (Bee, 1996; Brookfield, 1986; Taylor and Marienau, 1995). Teachers of adults want their learning connected to the here and now, to integrate into their daily lives, to make sense, and to have meaning for them.

Two other areas need to be considered when we look to adult learners and understand their characteristics. The area of adult development provides us with much information about how adults age and physically change throughout the life span. It is important to consider these physical and psychological changes and adaptations as we plan and deliver programs. Our expectations of adults' physical and psychological attributes need to be adjusted to align with what recent research tells us about aging. We now know that education, learning, and keeping active lead to increased quality of life in one's later years (Bee, 2000). This research refutes the idea that "you can't teach an old dog new tricks." The second area is socioeconomics. It is essential to understand how social and cultural contexts influence education. Whether we consider the gender and racial biases that have challenged teachers of adults or address access issues for opportunities, equipment, materials, and technology, we need to reflect critically on our assumptions and their ethnocentric biases.

Principles of Adult Learning

Ideas and concepts of adult learning have been evolving over the years as practitioners and researchers have observed adults learning in various contexts, throughout the life span, and with differing goals and motivations. Although there is consensus among many on the central principles to guide us in understanding the process of adult learning and planning educational programs, Merriam and Caffarella (1999) also stress the importance of the interaction of the learner with the sociocultural context and the learning process. It is important to take into consideration the characteristics of the adult learner, the context in which adult learning is occurring, and the process through which we deliver education and training each time we approach professional development. These unique features set the conditions for our planning and provide the meaning frameworks for our adult learners.

We also can rely on the rich resources of the field of adult education to guide us in our work with teachers of adults. Lawler and King (2000) present six adult learning principles to guide professional developers: "create a climate of respect, encourage active participation, build on experience, employ collaborative inquiry, learn for action, and empower the participants" (pp. 21–22). Each of these principles is grounded in the literature and practice of adult education. Lawler and King find it important to apply these principles in professional development in order to ensure effective programming and transfer of learning. In the following paragraphs, each of these principles is elaborated on in the context of working with teachers of adults.

Create a Climate of Respect. This principle, grounded in humanistic philosophy and sound organizational theory (Elias and Merriam, 1995; Galbraith, 1998), encourages us to start where the learner is by taking into consideration the characteristics, values, and educational goals the teacher of adults brings to the professional development activity. A climate of respect is created when both the social and physical environments are conducive to adult learning. This requires us to acknowledge the characteristics of our learners, their learning styles, their educational background and experiences, and their professional development goals. We must incorporate our understanding of these characteristics, styles, and experiences into the design and delivery of the professional development program. In particular, we must understand the unique characteristics of teachers of adults in their roles and responsibilities in their various settings.

Encourage Active Participation. Once we have created a climate of respect, we need to hear from our teachers of adults and ensure their participation in every phase of our programming. These individuals are accustomed to taking charge in their daily lives. Their professional responsibilities demand them to be active in their organizations as they make decisions on program and curriculum content, assess student and participant learning, and seek new ways to work with their adult students. Being respectful of their professional expertise by inviting their participation and collaboration encourages learning. Elsewhere I suggest, "Adults learn more effectively and efficiently when they actively participate in the educational activity" (Lawler, 1991, p. 39). Engaging the teacher of adults in active interchange from the very start creates goodwill and a cooperative environment.

Build on Experience. Rousseau considered the student a blank slate. As educators of adults we are very much aware that our students—adult learners—are anything but blank slates. Adult learners come to education with a wealth of experience, and teachers of adults are no exception. These learners are especially experienced in education, a valuable quality when incorporating their active participation in a professional development setting. But this experience can also be a barrier, because many of them—many of us—have had poor and ineffectual learning experiences. We cannot divorce a learner's past experience from the present educational event. Adults bring their worldviews based on their personal histories with them to the learning event (Apps, 1991). This will influence their acceptance of information and affect how learning occurs. Professional developers working with teachers of adults can take advantage of these factors and build on the experience for positive transfer of learning. For example, teachers of adults can share their success stories with one another as the opening exercise for a professional development day.

Employ Collaborative Inquiry. Our educational system has been built on an individualist framework, and most teachers see themselves working in isolation. However, educators have been aware for some time now of the value of cooperative and collaborative learning and planning (Caffarella, 2002). Participants can collaborate in assessing needs, work in small groups in the classroom, and alternate education roles in establishing objectives and goals (Brookfield, 1986). Because of their own experiences, teachers of adults can be a valuable resource in a collaborative effort to create and deliver a professional development program. Although additional effort may be needed to engage teachers of adults in shifting from their old educational paradigms, collaborative inquiry can be an effective tool for enhancing their motivation for professional development.

Learn for Action. As we saw earlier, adults are interested in immediately applying their learning and making connections between their educational experiences and their lives. We can incorporate the teacher of adults' experience and educational goals into our professional development so that learning can be taken out of the classroom and put to use in a practical and thoughtful way. If we see professional development for teachers of adults as an opportunity to motivate them to consider, implement, and promote new ideas, instructional processes, and learning paradigms, then we need to incorporate action plans in this process. To learn for action means to be guided for application, to understand the connections between content and application, and to have opportunities in the professional development setting and afterward to take action on learning. Assuming that learners will take action on their learning and will use the information presented after reflection is crucial for change to take place (Cranton, 1997; Mezirow and Associates, 1990).

Empower the Participants. Reflecting and taking action based on learning empowers the adult learner (Cranton, 1997). If the goals of adult education and professional development are change and growth, then opportunities and strategies that empower the learner are essential. This principle is based on the belief that adults are capable of understanding a range of possibilities and have the ability to make choices based on this awareness and understanding (Brookfield, 1986). If individuals are able to influence and change their environment as a result of an educational experience, they have been empowered. Because most professional development activities are concerned with changing some aspect of the status quo, it is essential to empower the teacher of adults to take action and make those changes after the activity is over.

With principles of adult learning in hand, we are now ready to be empowered ourselves and take action as we consider the professional development of teachers of adults. Each principle does not stand alone but is connected with an educational philosophy that values the teacher of adults as an adult learner with the capacity to change and grow. If we follow these principles, it demonstrates our commitment to collaboration and respect.

Adult Learning Model for Faculty Development

Incorporating adult learning principles into our professional development activities and viewing teachers of adults as adult learners may be a paradigm shift for us. Whether we have been creating professional development for these participants for many years or are novices at this new venture, we bring with us our own backgrounds and experiences as both educators and adult learners. Specific examples of incorporating such adult learning principles in professional development activities can be found in recent writings (Lawler and King, 2000; Licklider, Schnelker, and Fulton, 1997–98; Smylie, 1995).

One model that is helpful for professional developers working with teachers of adults is the Adult Learning Model for Faculty Development (Lawler and King, 2000). This model incorporates both the principles of adult learning and well-grounded adult education program-planning concepts. The four stages of the model—preplanning, planning, delivery, and follow-up—are interrelated and dynamic. At each stage, we ask how the activities and proposed learning objectives are compatible with the adult learning principles. As professional developers we are continually asked if we are taking teachers of adults into consideration, if we know their needs and goals, if we are certain of strategies for immediate action, and if we can elicit their collaboration not only in the class itself but also in the planning and evaluation processes. Although the model encourages us to keep the teacher of adults at the forefront, it also provides an opportunity to reflect on our practice and critique our own assumptions about learning, the participants, and the goals for the activities in an organizational context and social milieu. As I present the model, I suggest critical questions to be asked and tasks to be completed at each stage, in order to direct professional developers in their planning. In addition, these paragraphs offer several examples of how each stage of the model can be incorporated into professional development for teachers of adults.

Preplanning. Even before we begin the formal planning for our teachers of adults, we need to address several questions: the purpose of the professional development initiative, how it fits in the culture, mission, and goals of the organization where the teachers are working with adult learners, and what resources are available to support the initiative. In answering these questions we begin our preplanning tasks. For example, as Maria, the director of an ESL program, begins to think about the annual retreat for her ESL teachers, she needs to understand her organizational culture, be clear about the role she will play as professional developer, assess her ESL teachers' needs, look for resources to support the program, and establish her goals. The answers will help set the overall direction for Maria to proceed with the professional development activity.

Planning. Getting down to specifics, several questions need to be asked during this second stage. Based on our resources, goals, and needs assessment, we can seek answers to questions about the type of professional development activities we need to design, who will be involved, and how we will schedule, promote, and deliver the program. Phil is planning three workshops on integrating Web-based learning in higher education for his adjunct faculty at the community college. As he considers possible questions from the intended participants, he begins the tasks of this second stage by seeking out faculty and colleagues who can act as resources, consultants, and sounding boards. Once he has this group, and his needs assessment, Phil is ready to select the specific topic, identify the presenter, and set the schedule. He can also look for ways to support the adjunct faculty in implementing their new learning and begin to think about evaluation, both during and after the program.

Delivery. At this stage we are interested in how all our planning can be incorporated and monitored. There are other questions about promoting the program and how well we incorporate adult learning principles into the actual delivery of the event. For example, as the time draws near for a customer service training program, the director of training and development at an investment company reviews her tasks. Alisha's preplanning and planning preparation is the solid foundation on which she will continue to build. She makes sure her promotional materials are in place. Her presenters are well-versed in adult learning principles, and she has planned a schedule to monitor the program through its completion.

Follow-Up. With the program over, we tend not to focus on this final stage in professional development. Yet it can be valuable for both the professional developer and the teacher of adults. Although we began to think of final evaluation plans earlier in the planning process, now is the time to put the plans into action. When the teachers of adults leave the program, what processes are in place to support their new skills and learning? Another question that needs to be answered at this stage is what we, as faculty developers, can gain from reflecting on our role in this endeavor (Lawler and King, 2000). Returning to Phil, now that his programs are over we see him reviewing evaluations from the adjunct faculty who attended his Web-based workshops. He also reflects on his own observations and perception of the event. Assessing his role in the process and what he learned will help him plan future events. Phil's task now is to ensure that the faculty have access to continued learning and support for their efforts as they incorporate the information and skills they gained at the workshops.

As most of us in professional development know, planning is not a linear process. We do many tasks at the same time while preparing and delivering our programs. Used as a guide, this model reminds us to view our teachers of adults as adult learners at all stages of the professional development process. For instance, we need the participation of the teachers of adults in our professional development activities. This model encourages us to view their participation as more than just showing up for the course or workshop. Participation is key throughout the planning, delivery, and evaluation processes. Teachers of adults' experiences and needs are also used as a foundation. The model provides a framework for going beyond a single professional development event and using the activities as building blocks for continued initiatives with teachers of adults.

Conclusion

Providing professional development for teachers of adults is a challenging and rewarding experience. Although their contexts may vary from a college campus to a factory workroom, these teachers are required to continue their own learning to stay current in their field, incorporate technology, remain certified, grow professionally, and even keep their jobs. Professional development activities can be worthwhile and useful; they can enhance growth. Or they can be boring, time-consuming, and irrelevant. If we look at professional development as an adult education activity, and at teachers of adults as adult learners, it increases our ability to ensure a positive and useful experience for those we teach.

References

Apps, J. W. *Mastering the Teaching of Adults.* Malabar, Fla.: Krieger, 1991.

Bee, H. L. *The Journey of Adulthood.* (3rd ed.) Upper Saddle River, N.J.: Prentice Hall, 1996.

Bee, H. L. *The Journey of Adulthood.* (4th ed.) Upper Saddle River, N.J.: Prentice Hall, 2000.

Brookfield, S. B. *Understanding and Facilitating Adult Learning.* San Francisco: Jossey-Bass, 1986.

Brookfield, S. B. *Becoming a Critically Reflective Teacher.* San Francisco: Jossey-Bass, 1995.

Caffarella, R. S. *Planning Programs for Adult Learners: A Practical Guide for Educators, Trainers, and Staff Developers.* (2nd ed.) San Francisco: Jossey-Bass, 2002.

Cranton, P. *Working with Adult Learners.* Middletown, Ohio: Wall & Emerson, 1992.

Cranton, P. (ed.). *Transformative Learning in Action: Insights from Practice.* New Directions for Adult and Continuing Education, no. 74. San Francisco: Jossey-Bass, 1997.

Elias, J. L., and Merriam, S. B. *Philosophical Foundations of Adult Education.* (2nd ed.) Malabar, Fla.: Krieger, 1995.

Galbraith, M. W. (ed.). *Adult Learning Methods.* (2nd ed.) Malabar, Fla.: Krieger, 1998.

Kolb, D. A. *Experiential Learning: Experience as the Source of Learning and Development.* Upper Saddle River, N.J.: Prentice Hall, 1984.

Lawler, P. A. *The Keys to Adult Learning: Theory and Practical Strategies.* Philadelphia: Research for Better Schools, 1991.

Lawler, P. A., and King, K. P. *Planning for Effective Faculty Development: Using Adult Learning Strategies.* Malabar, Fla.: Krieger, 2000.

Licklider, B. E., Schnelker, D. L., and Fulton, C. "Revisioning Faculty Development for Changing Times: The Foundation and Framework." *Journal of Staff, Program, and Organizational Development,* 1997–98, *15*(3), 121–133.

Merriam, S. B., and Caffarella, R. S. *Learning in Adulthood.* (2nd ed.) San Francisco: Jossey-Bass, 1999.

Mezirow, J., and Associates. *Fostering Critical Reflection in Adulthood: A Guide to Transformative and Emancipatory Learning.* San Francisco: Jossey-Bass, 1990.

Smith, D. M., and Kolb, D. A. *User's Guide for the Learning Style Inventory.* Boston: McBer, 1986.

Smylie, M. A. "Teacher Learning in the Workplace: Implications for School Reform." In T. R. Guskey and M. Huberman (eds.), *Professional Development in Education: New Paradigms and Practices.* New York: Teachers College Press, 1995.

Taylor, K., and Marienau, C. (eds.). *Learning Environments for Women's Adult Development: Bridges Toward Change.* New Directions for Adult and Continuing Education, no. 65. San Francisco: Jossey-Bass, 1995.

Taylor, K., Marienau, C., and Fiddler, M. *Developing Adult Learners: Strategies for Teachers and Trainers.* San Francisco: Jossey-Bass, 2000.

PATRICIA A. LAWLER is a professor in the Center for Education, Widener University, Chester, Pennsylvania.

3

This chapter discusses how to create learner-centered approaches to teacher development by analyzing educators' teaching and learning orientations as well as their career stages.

A Case for Learner-Centered Teaching and Learning

Barbara J. Daley

Recently I had the opportunity to participate in two different teacher development programs. In the first, I was awarded grant funds to convert an existing course to an on-line format. As part of this grant, I was to participate in seminars on the use of technology in teaching and learning. In the second, I was funded to conduct a classroom research project under the Scholarship of Teaching and Learning (SOTL) program that is under way on our campus (see http://www.uwm.edu/Dept/CIPD/Programs/SOT&L/CarnegieOverview.html). In this second program I also participated in seminars with other campus colleagues working on SOTL projects. Both programs were well-planned and well-implemented. They also appeared to offer me the opportunity I was looking for to increase my classroom research activities as well as the opportunity to learn more about the use of technology in teaching and learning.

But in the first program I found myself mentally and physically "checking out." After a while, I was skipping the meetings, not participating, and mostly, just working on designing my on-line course. In contrast, I found myself eagerly awaiting the time when the next seminar would be conducted for the second program. I looked forward to the work with my colleagues, to our discussions, and to the interactions. Reflecting on my reactions to these programs, I started to wonder, "What is the difference here?" Both were good, solid programs designed to meet learning needs I had expressed. "Why," I wondered, "do I react so differently to these programs?" It appeared that the teaching and learning approaches used to plan the programs, along with the career stages of the educators enrolled in each program, combined to cause my reactions.

NEW DIRECTIONS FOR ADULT AND CONTINUING EDUCATION, no. 98, Summer 2003 © Wiley Periodicals, Inc.

Thus, I believe that the way I reacted to these two different teacher development programs is based on an understanding of (1) learning orientations, (2) teaching orientations, and (3) career stages of teachers in professional development programs. In this chapter, I will discuss these three parameters and then extrapolate strategies to develop learner-centered models of teacher professional development.

Learning Orientations

Learning orientations are the first element to affect the development of learner-centered models for professional development of teachers. Merriam and Caffarella (1999) have grouped a variety of learning theories into five topical areas that they call orientations to learning: *behaviorist, cognitivist, humanist, social,* and *constructivist.* Each is framed by a particular group of learning theories that reflect the purpose of education, a different view of the learning process and the locus of learning, and a specific manner in which the teacher functions in this orientation.

The first orientation to learning, according to Merriam and Caffarella (1999), is the behaviorist orientation. Behaviorists (Skinner, 1974; Thorndike, Bregman, Tilton, and Woodyard, 1928) believe that for learning to occur there must be a change in behavior; thus, the purpose of education is to produce the desired behavioral change. In this view, the external environment can be arranged to produce behavioral change through the use of reinforcements that reward learners for what the teacher wants them to continue doing. The role of the teacher, then, is to develop an environment that will encourage the learners to demonstrate the desired response.

Merriam and Caffarella (1999) describe their second orientation to learning as cognitivist. Cognitivists (Ausubel, Novak, and Hanesian, 1986; Novak and Gowin, 1984) focus on the internal mental processes of learning. For them, the purpose of education is to help the learner develop skills needed to learn better. Unlike the behaviorists, cognitivists believe that what is important in learning is the manner in which learners are making connections, processing information, and thinking about the material they are studying. The role of the teacher in a cognitive orientation is to structure the content of the learning activity and help the learner develop the ability to think and process information in new ways.

The third learning orientation is humanist. Humanists (Rogers, 1983) believe that the purpose of education is to assist the learner to develop into a fully functioning, self-actualized human being. Therefore, the role of the teacher in this framework is to facilitate the development of the entire person through a focus on life experiences, affective needs, personal growth, and personal development. In a humanist framework, teachers focus on self-directed learning leading to individual growth and change.

Social learning is the fourth orientation to learning. According to this school of thought, learning occurs through the interaction of the person, the person's behavior, and the environment (Bandura, 1986). Through the process of observation and imitation, the learner sees others working in a particular fashion and tries on that role. The purpose of education in a social learning framework is to model new roles and behaviors. Thus, the teacher becomes the guide for this role-modeling process. Social learning is seen in mentoring, preceptor, apprenticeship, and internship programs.

The final orientation to learning is constructivist. Constructivists (Dewey, 1938; Piaget, 1966) believe that individuals create knowledge by linking new information with past experiences to create a personal process for meaning-making. In a constructivist framework, the learner progressively differentiates concepts into more and more complex understandings while reconciling new abstractions with concrete knowledge learned from previous experience (Novak, 1998). Learners make new knowledge meaningful by linking it to previous experience and their changing environment.

When we look at the multiplicity of learning orientations, we can see that teachers in a professional development program may learn in a variety of ways. Some may prefer a behavioral learning approach, and others may prefer a constructivist approach. In addition, teachers from different disciplines in higher education may lean more toward one learning orientation than the others. Thus it is vital that we consider the learning orientation of educators in professional development programs.

Teaching Orientations

We also need to consider teaching orientations in developing learner-centered models for teacher professional development. Based on his extensive research, Pratt (1998) describes five different perspectives on teaching. He calls these different teaching perspectives: *transmission, apprenticeship, development, nurturing,* and *social reform.* Pratt indicates that a variety of perspectives on teaching are needed and that these perspectives should "recognize diversity within teachers, learners, content, context, ideals, and purposes" (1998, p. 4).

According to Pratt, content is paramount in the transmission perspective. These teachers consider themselves experts in their subject matter and see their role in the teaching-learning interaction as conveyors of content. The focus here is on how the teacher plans, organizes, and delivers content (Alstete, 2000).

Pratt describes the second perspective, the apprenticeship orientation, as one where the teacher and content are closely linked to a particular context of practice. Here the teacher helps the learner not only to understand the content but also to assume the role in which the content will be carried out. Teaching from this perspective encompasses acting as a role model and demonstrating how content is used in a particular context.

Pratt describes the third teaching orientation as developmental, which differs from the previous two in that it focuses on the learner. Although the apprenticeship and transmission orientations emphasize the relationship of the teacher and the content, the developmental perspective stresses the relationship between the learner and the content. As Pratt indicates, "Content is the means through which preferred ways of thinking are developed" (1998, p. 47). Those educators teaching from the developmental perspective focus on helping learners solve problems, using their prior knowledge to create new ways of thinking, and fostering the creation of meaning for the individual learner.

Pratt's fourth orientation, the nurturing perspective, centers on the relationship between the teacher and the learner because this relationship is critical in fostering the development of the learner's personal growth and self-esteem (Knowles, 1984). Thus, the connection between learner and teacher is paramount, and the role of content is as the vehicle though which this nurturing relationship is developed.

Finally, Pratt discusses the social reform perspective, which focuses on the ideals of social change and social reform. Learners and content are often less important than the broader social agenda and the purpose of the educational offering.

In summary, Pratt organizes teaching into varying perspectives. The relative importance of the learner, teacher, content, context, and ideals changes in each. One of the challenges in changing how we teach is understanding the perspective, or combination of perspectives, from which we operate. As Pratt states, "If we wish to understand and influence peoples' teaching, we must go beneath the surface to consider the intentions and beliefs related to teaching and learning which inform their assumptions" (1998, p. 11).

Career Stages

The third element affecting participants in teacher development programs is career stage. Teachers come to professional development programs with a wide range of teaching and other professional experiences. In many professional development programs, career stage is a small consideration in program planning or is not considered at all. Yet we know from the professional development literature that as individuals develop in their careers they move through distinct stages. Dreyfus and Dreyfus (1985) explained that professionals move through five stages of professional development, which they labeled *novice, advanced beginner, competent, proficient,* and *expert.* In each stage the professional develops more and more autonomy and creativity, relying less and less on formal structures and rules. Previous studies with pilots and nurses (Benner, 1984; Dreyfus and Dreyfus, 1985) have indicated that because novices enter their professional world with so little experience, they tend to rely on rules or instructions. New teachers in the novice stage, for example, often teach in the manner in which they were taught. In the advanced beginner and competent stages, professionals begin to recognize the validity of their experiences and become aware of a plan of action as they develop their ability to cope with unpredictable situations. As professionals move into the proficient stage, they develop a more holistic sense of their work. Such individuals are able to see the larger picture of their work and understand how their day-to-day actions contribute to the picture, including their students and their organizations.

Finally, experts have developed a great deal of commonsense understanding of their work that is based on a "deep web of perspectives that causes them to view a situation in terms of past situations. Thus, the expert has learned to expect certain events and even selectively to attend to certain aspects of the situation" (Benner and Tanner, 1987, p. 28). Among expert teachers, one sees a highly developed understanding of their discipline and the content they teach. In addition, these teachers demonstrate the ability to connect with their learners in a specific context to facilitate learning.

A professional's career stage is also important because, as previous studies indicate (Daley, 1999), professionals at different career stages learn differently. Novice professionals tend to rely on a more contingent learning process; because they are still striving to understand their role, they will often learn what others say they should learn in the way others say they should learn it. Experts, however, tend to rely more on constructivist learning strategies. In other words, experts tend to learn by differentiating and integrating new information with their experiences. Moreover, experts often understand their own learning and are confident in their ability to learn and grow in their chosen profession.

Reflecting on Teacher Development Experiences

In analyzing the two teacher development programs in which I recently participated, I came to believe that the programs were operated so differently because the assumptions about learning orientations, teaching orientations, and career stages that were behind each of them were different too (see Table 3.1).

As Table 3.1 indicates, the first program focused mostly on content. The assumption was that teachers needed to learn about different kinds of technology before they could apply it to their own course. Thus the learning orientation was mostly behavioral, and the content was presented in a

Table 3.1. Comparison of Teacher Development Programs

Elements of Teacher Development Programs	Program One: Technology	Program Two: SOTL
Learning orientation	Behavioral, cognitive	Constructivist
Teaching orientation	Transmission	Developmental, nurturing
Career stage	Novice	Expert

transmission orientation to teaching. Finally, teachers were assumed to be mostly novices in their approach to using technology in teaching.

The second program focused on cross-disciplinary colleague relationships while conducting SOTL projects. It was assumed that the prior knowledge of teachers would guide the projects, research, and dialogue. Therefore, the learning orientation was more constructivist and the teaching orientation was more developmental and nurturing. Finally, those planning the second program assumed that the teachers participating had a high level of expertise and were competent to make their own learning decisions.

I believe that I reacted differently to each program because, in my mind, the second was created around a learner-centered approach to teacher professional development. The second program honored the fact that teachers know how to learn, know how to find the information they need, and know how to link it to their practice. It supported the teachers' need to converse with peers and connect new learning to previous experiences. Finally, the SOTL development program was designed by people who understood me and the context in which I worked as a teacher. It was apparent that the program centered on the role of teachers and existed to support educators' work in both teaching and scholarship.

Strategies to Support Learner-Centered Approaches

From the previous discussion, it is clear that I believe a learner-centered approach to teacher development is contingent on the integration of learning orientation, teaching orientation, and career stage. Thus, I believe that teachers of adults can use the following three strategies to enhance their efforts to develop learner-centered classrooms.

Examine Your Own Beliefs About Teaching and Learning. As a person developing programs for teachers, it is important that you understand your own views about teaching and learning. Often these views are not explicit, yet they will be embedded in any professional development program you create. Understanding which approach to learning you tend to favor, and which teaching orientation you often rely on, will allow you to understand your usual approach and will foster more creativity in expanding your orientations to teaching and learning. Numerous assessments can be helpful in this process. For example, Dan Pratt's Web site has a teaching perspective inventory that can help you examine your own beliefs (http://www.edst.educ.ubc.ca/pratt.html). The developmental teaching and constructivist learning orientations seem to offer the theoretical frameworks fostering a learner-centered approach to teacher development programs.

Analyze the Career Level of Participating Educators. Often, professional development programs—including those for teachers—are created for novice practitioners. These programs provide information with the assumption that educators will take it and use it in their teaching. But experts learn more effectively through dialogue and analysis of previous experiences in light of new learning. With this in mind, be sure to consider the career stages of your audience when developing learner-centered approaches to teacher development. As a guide, Weston and McAlpine (2001) offer a three-phase continuum that includes growth in teaching, dialogue, and growth in scholarship as approaches to analyzing career states of teaching.

Develop Strategies to Support Knowledge Construction and Development of Meaning. Ausubel (Ausubel, Novak, and Hanesian, 1986) states that the most fundamental element in creating a learner-centered approach is "what the learner already knows. Ascertain this and teach him accordingly" (p. iv). Developing this learner-centered approach, then, relies on strategies to promote a conceptual understanding of the content and methods to link with learners' previous experience. Concept maps (Novak, 1998; Novak and Gowin, 1984), discussion (Brookfield and Preskill, 1999), and dialogue (Mezirow, 1990; Mezirow and Associates, 2000) are all strategies that can support this approach. Finally, an added focus on developing reflective understanding can benefit teacher development programs, because this reflection encourages the learner to link past and previous experiences with new information in a constructivist orientation. Such strategies as critical incidents (Brookfield, 1995), journals (Boud, 2001; Mezirow, 1990), and teaching autobiographies (Dominice, 1990) can be helpful in this process.

Conclusion

In summary, creating learner-centered approaches to teacher development will require attention to learning orientation, teaching orientation, and career stage of educators. The power in these learner-centered approaches is that they help develop the ability to learn from experience, to integrate knowledge, and to think reflectively. The hope is that as teachers experience learner-centered classrooms in their own professional development they will in turn develop more learner-centered classrooms with their students. This will mean that educators of adults can benefit from the strategies outlined here. Adopting a learner-centered approach will require changes in the way we think, the way we teach adults, and the way we organize our professional development programs. As Lawler and King (2000) indicate, "This call for change demands that we move away from a deficit model of development toward one of professional development and growth" (p. 6).

References

Alstete, J. "Post-Tenure Faculty Development: Building a System of Faculty Improvement and Appreciation." *ASHE ERIC Higher Education Report*, 2000, 27(4).

Ausubel, D. P., Novak, J. D., and Hanesian, H. *Educational Psychology: A Cognitive View.* (2nd ed.) New York: Werbel and Peck, 1986.

Bandura, A. *Social Foundations of Thought and Action: A Social Cognitive Theory.* Upper Saddle River, N.J.: Prentice Hall, 1986.

Benner, P. *From Novice to Expert: Excellence and Power in Clinical Nursing Practice.* Reading, Mass.: Addison-Wesley, 1984.

Benner, P., and Tanner, C. "Clinical Judgment: How Expert Nurses Use Intuition." *American Journal of Nursing,* 1987, *87,* 23–31.

Boud, D. "Using Journal Writing to Enhance Reflective Practice." In L. M. English and M. A. Gillen (eds.), *Promoting Journal Writing in Adult Education.* New Directions for Adult and Continuing Education, no. 90. San Francisco: Jossey-Bass, 2001.

Brookfield, S. *Becoming a Critically Reflective Teacher.* San Francisco: Jossey-Bass, 1995.

Brookfield, S., and Preskill, S. *Discussion as a Way of Teaching: Tools and Techniques for Democratic Classrooms.* San Francisco: Jossey-Bass, 1999.

Daley, B. "Novice to Expert: An Exploration of How Professionals Learn." *Adult Education Quarterly,* 1999, *49*(4), 133–147.

Dewey, J. *Experience and Education.* New York: Collier Books, 1938.

Dominice, P. F. "Composing Education Biographies: Group Reflection Through Life Histories." In J. Mezirow (ed.), *Fostering Critical Reflection in Adulthood.* San Francisco: Jossey-Bass, 1990.

Dreyfus, H., and Dreyfus, S. *Mind over Machine: The Power of Human Intuition and Expertise in the Era of the Computer.* New York: Free Press, 1985.

Knowles, M. S. *The Adult Learner: A Neglected Species.* (3rd ed.) Houston: Gulf, 1984.

Lawler, P. A., and King, K. P. *Planning for Effective Faculty Development: Using Adult Learning Strategies.* Malabar, Fla.: Krieger, 2000.

Merriam, S. B., and Caffarella, R. S. *Learning in Adulthood.* San Francisco: Jossey-Bass, 1999.

Mezirow, J. *Fostering Critical Reflection in Adulthood.* San Francisco: Jossey-Bass, 1990.

Mezirow, J., and Associates. *Learning as Transformation: Critical Perspectives on a Theory in Progress.* San Francisco: Jossey-Bass, 2000.

Novak, J. *Learning, Creating, and Using Knowledge: Concept Maps as Facilitative Tools in Schools and Corporations.* Mahwah, N.J.: Erlbaum, 1998.

Novak, J., and Gowin, B. *Learning How to Learn.* Cambridge: Cambridge University Press, 1984.

Piaget, M. *Psychology of Intelligence.* Totowa, N.J.: Littlefield, Adams, 1966.

Pratt, D. *Five Perspectives on Teaching in Adult and Higher Education.* Malabar, Fla.: Krieger, 1998.

Rogers, C. R. *Freedom to Learn for the '80s.* Columbus, Ohio: Merrill, 1983.

Skinner, B. F. *About Behaviorism.* New York: Knopf, 1974.

Thorndike, E. L., Bregman, E. O., Tilton, J. W., and Woodyard, E. *Adult Learning.* Old Tappan, N.J.: Macmillan, 1928.

Weston, C., and McAlpine, L. "Making Explicit the Development Toward the Scholarship of Teaching." In C. Kreber (ed.), *Scholarship Revisited: Perspectives on the Scholarship of Teaching.* New Directions for Teaching and Learning, no. 86. San Francisco: Jossey-Bass, 2001.

BARBARA J. DALEY is associate professor of adult and continuing education in the Department of Administrative Leadership at the University of Wisconsin-Milwaukee.

4

From the framework of transformative learning, this chapter explores how professional development can lead educators to be authentic, individuated, critically reflective practitioners. Practical strategies are provided.

Transformative Learning as a Professional Development Goal

Patricia Cranton, Kathleen P. King

Educators of adults are in a unique position among professionals in that they often have not had the opportunity to learn how to do their job. Most educators of adults come into their positions through a circuitous route, one that does not include teacher training. At some point in their careers, they may return to school, most often to study adult education on a part-time basis, but generally they learn their craft through experience, modeling themselves on others and reflecting on their practice. Professional development activities when they are available tend to be seen as not valuable, perhaps because they are not themselves grounded in adult learning theory. This chapter explores how professional developers may benefit from understanding and using transformative learning.

In his classic and influential work on understanding human interests and kinds of knowledge, Habermas (1971) identifies three kinds of knowledge: *instrumental or technical, communicative,* and *emancipatory.* In modern society, we have a tendency to value objective, scientific (or instrumental) knowledge over socially constructed knowledge. But knowledge about teaching is primarily communicative rather than instrumental. That is, it is about understanding ourselves, others, and the norms of the organization, community, and society in which we live. Professional development activities that focus on the *how to* rather than the broader issues of practice are an attempt to make knowledge about teaching instrumental. Inevitably, they fall short in meeting the needs of educators of adults because there is just so much more to learning about teaching. Knowledge about teaching is also emancipatory. It is about critically questioning and reflecting on what we do,

NEW DIRECTIONS FOR ADULT AND CONTINUING EDUCATION, no. 98, Summer 2003 © Wiley Periodicals, Inc.

how it works, and why we believe it is important (Brookfield, 1995; Cranton, 1996). This is the heart of transformative learning.

In this chapter, we briefly review transformative learning theory as it relates to professional development. We explore how transformative learning helps us become authentic and individuated teachers, the kind of teachers who are conscious of and questioning of our habits of mind. We discuss the nature of critical reflection on teaching, and finally and perhaps most important, we outline strategies for transformative professional development.

Transformative Learning Theory

Transformative learning theory has now been with us for over twenty-five years. Since Mezirow's (1975, 1978) initial introduction of the concept of transformation into the adult education literature, the theory has grown, been elaborated on, challenged, and in recent years, received considerable attention in both the academic community and the world of practice (Merriam and Caffarella, 1999; Taylor, 1998). At its core, the idea is elegant in its simplicity. We make meaning of the world through our experiences. What happens once, we expect to happen again. Through this process, we develop habits of mind or a frame of reference for understanding the world, much of which is uncritically assimilated. In the process of daily living, we absorb values, assumptions, and beliefs about how things are without much thought.

When something different happens, we can be led to question our way of seeing the world. We ask, "What happened here?" and "How did I come to think this way?" and "Why is this important?" This questioning, or critical self-reflection, may not be linear or sequential or appear at the time to be logical, but it is essentially a rational process of seeing that our previously held views no longer fit—they are too narrow, too limiting, and do not explain the new experience. Given that we are social creatures, we most likely discuss this process with others, or as Mezirow says, we engage in discourse (Mezirow and Associates, 2000). Ideas and evidence from others help us to consider our own views in a new light.

Transformative learning takes place when this process leads us to open up our frame of reference, discard a habit of mind, see alternatives, and thereby act differently in the world (Mezirow and Associates, 2000). When educators are led to examine their practice critically and thereby acquire alternative ways of understanding what they do, transformative learning about teaching takes place (Cranton, 1996). It seems that this must be a goal of professional development. If we do not consciously think about and reflect on our practice, we become nothing more than automatons following a dubious set of rules or principles—rules or principles that are unlikely to be relevant in the ever-changing, complex context of teaching and learning.

Transformation, Individuation, and Authenticity

Jung ([1921] 1971) describes a lifelong process of *individuation*—the development of the whole person, indivisible and yet distinct from the general, collective psychology. Although the construct of individuation includes other intriguing concepts, for our purposes here we focus on the way in which we come to have a sense of self that differentiates us from others. Educators who question the values of the organization they work for, or resign when they no longer fit in, are realizing that their views are separate from those of the organization. Breaking away, grouping, and regrouping with more like-minded others continues throughout the lifetime as we continue refining who we are. Without individuation we have no foundation on which to question assumptions and norms because we cannot see ourselves as separate from those norms.

Authenticity is the expression of the genuine self in the community (Cranton, 2001). Teaching is a specialized form of communication that has as its goal the promotion of learning. Good communication is based on authenticity. If we communicate through a persona, we create a barrier to communication and hence to effective teaching.

Individuation, authenticity, and transformation form a sort of spiraling journey for the educator. Individuation is a prerequisite for transformative learning. We must be able to see ourselves as differentiated from the collective in order to question its norms. At the same time, individuation is a transformative process. In differentiating our self from others, we see where our values are different from and the same as those of others. Transformative learning leads to further individuation as we separate ourselves from the community whose values we no longer share. Transformative learning also leads back to authenticity as we express our views in the community. Being authentic leads to further transformation and individuation. We no longer run with the herd; we make choices based on who we are. The spiral moves upward.

Meaningful professional development must go far beyond learning to use a new piece of software or a new trick for increasing student participation. It must involve educators as whole persons—their values, beliefs, and assumptions about teaching and their ways of seeing the world.

Habits of Mind About Teaching

As is the case with all of our frames of reference, our ways of understanding the world, our habits of mind about teaching, are absorbed as we experience life. We acquire values and assumptions about teaching from the community and society we live in, from the institution we work in, and from family, friends, and colleagues. Our ideas about teaching are also shaped by who we are as people, our personal preferences, and our personalities.

The society and community in which we live have powerful norms about education and the role of the educator. At one time educators of adults were seen to be subversive agents, inciting the masses to revolution by giving them the power of knowledge (Selman, 1989). Today, education may be viewed as a way of promoting good citizenship, socializing people to fit into a profession or organization, providing the building blocks of democracy, improving productivity, cultivating future leaders, and freeing people from oppression. We encounter these and many other conflicting social norms about education daily. As we make our own meaning of the world, we are influenced by the norms implicitly or explicitly presented to us, even often assimilating them uncritically.

The institution or organization in which we practice also has its culture of teaching. A faculty of nursing may promote socialization of nurses into the profession or encourage critical thought and autonomy. A large corporation may see the role of human resource development to be one of empowering staff or fostering acceptance of the corporate vision. As educators, we may fall into the culture of our workplace without much thought or we may question it and work to change it.

Our own personal experiences with education and our basic teaching and learning preferences shape our habits of mind about teaching in many ways. We may model ourselves on teachers we admired in childhood. We may teach the way we prefer to learn ourselves. Persons who value structure and organization in their daily lives may be organized teachers. Persons who are intuitive, creative, and innovative may carry those characteristics into their teaching. Again, we often tend not to question these things—we teach based on what we have experienced and who we are.

Effective professional development brings our habits of mind about teaching into consciousness and allows us to examine critically what we believe and value in our work as educators. The goal is to open up alternatives, introduce new ways of thinking about teaching—a goal that is potentially transformative.

Critical Self-Reflection on Teaching

Professional development, to help educators understand what they do and why they do it, needs to incorporate activities that foster content, process, and premise reflection. If we are to encourage critical self-reflection on our habits of mind about teaching, it is helpful to look at the process in more detail. Mezirow (1991) outlines three ways in which we interpret experience through reflection.

Content reflection is the examination of the content or description of a problem. At the end of a less-than-successful class or workshop, we ask ourselves, "What happened here?" or "What did I do that led to that outcome?" We might review what we said or think about the nature of the interactions between participants.

Process reflection involves checking on the problem-solving strategies we are using. We ask, "Am I overlooking something?" or "Do I not understand the learning styles of my students?" We look for ways in which our thinking may have gone wrong.

Premise reflection is the questioning of the problem itself. We might ask, "Why do I feel responsible for this situation?" or "Does it really matter that everyone did not have a good learning experience today?" It is premise reflection that has the potential to lead to transformation of our meaning perspectives.

There is little point in adding another technique to our collection if we do not comprehend why we are doing so. Critical self-reflection on teaching can be a starting point for continuing, self-directed professional development.

Strategies for Transformative Professional Development

Research, literature, and practice indicate strategies that may be applied to professional development in order to promote or encourage critical questioning and potentially transformative learning. We include five strategies here: *action plans, reflective activities, case studies, curriculum development,* and *critical theory discussions.* These strategies may be specifically adapted to most settings, including face-to-face and distance learning.

Through both action plans for themselves and reflective activities for their educator students, developers lay out the sequence of events for the professional development session or program and build toward reflection and application. Action plans (King, 2003) that include reflective activities may be used by the developer to guide the flow of presentation, dialogue, and learning. This integration of methods can be accomplished as the developer explicitly poses questions about meaning, assumptions, perspectives, and application. In addition to guiding the developer, action plans have at least two additional benefits: they help learners become familiar with critical reflection on their profession through practice and modeling, and they may be used to guide loosely, but not dictate, the teaching and learning experience. Although action plans can give form to our activities, they can also help us to consider new directions or needs of learners (educators) without losing our bearings or becoming sidetracked in less productive ways.

Case studies, a third strategy described by Marsick (1998), are used to provide an effective focus for reflection on practice (Schön, 1987). By considering real-life examples, educators of adults can be guided to recognize the harder questions, to probe unspoken assumptions, and to analyze the consequences of choices and actions. By working in groups to analyze, synthesize, and make recommendations, educators enter a virtual laboratory where they try out new possible responses and enter into dialogue with their partners about meaning, purposes, and possibilities. When groups are given intriguing cases and a short list of starting questions they can enter into meaningful discussion of the philosophical and practical aspects of their craft. Developers may monitor or visit the small groups to facilitate group dynamics or respond to questions.

Like many adult learners, educators thrive on the application of their learning. A fourth powerful strategy to link theory and practice emerges from curriculum development through professional development. For instance, developers can use integrative curriculum development as a capstone activity for sessions that introduce new teaching styles or methods. Rather than uncritically accepting new techniques and viewing them as instrumental knowledge about teaching, educators can explore, discuss, practice, and prepare new material that is relevant to their classes. Transformative learning can occur when educators have the opportunity to test a new perspective in this powerful manner. Juxtaposing new concepts and practice on the old becomes action rather than just theory with curriculum development. Moving from learning about concepts to operationalizing them brings many new insights that may be furthered through later discussions once the educators have tried the materials they created.

Higher education has traditionally prized the essence of critical theory (Merriam and Caffarella, 1999) in lively discourse among scholars as they carefully step outside of their own predispositions to reexamine facts, evidence, reasoning, and arguments. In fact, the age-old perspective of higher education institutions being learning communities of scholars underscores this practice (Rudolph, 1990). Professional development programs for educators of adults can build on this practice by using analysis and discourse in their teaching and learning practice. For example, faculty can be guided to consider how their students use Internet sources. Using a "Web quest" worksheet, they visit a variety of sites to make observations and come to realize that not all information posted on the Internet is factual (Alexander and Tate, 1999; King, 2003). In group discussion they then look at how this situation can benefit the learning process, and the educators usually begin to connect it with opportunities to build critical thinking skills, critical theory, evaluation, and analysis. Educators are not only critically examining the purposes and meaning of information but are also being guided to question their purposes and meaning in selecting and providing information for their classes. When professional developers engage educators of adults in dialogue about their thoughts and questions, such critically reflective practice can lead the educators to challenging exchanges and the construction of new understanding.

Conclusion

If we view professional development as an opportunity to cultivate transformative learning it gives us a new perspective on our goals, what we do in our practice, and how we think about our work. Through programs and activities that encourage educators of adults to become authentic and individuated teachers, doors of new possibilities open. Rather than teaching and learning as usual, they can begin to look at their habits of mind and work with new questions, insight, and promise. Professional development that is transformative in nature provides grounding for continued lifelong learning in the professions.

References

Alexander, J., and Tate, M. A. *Web Wisdom: How to Evaluate and Create Information Quality on the Web.* Mahwah, N.J.: Erlbaum, 1999.

Brookfield, S. *Becoming a Critically Reflective Teacher.* San Francisco: Jossey-Bass, 1995.

Cranton, P. *Professional Development as Transformative Learning.* San Francisco: Jossey-Bass, 1996.

Cranton, P. *Becoming an Authentic Teacher in Higher Education.* Malabar, Fla.: Krieger, 2001.

Habermas, J. *Kinds of Human Interests and Knowledge.* Boston: Beacon Press, 1971.

Jung, C. *Psychological Types.* Princeton, N.J.: Princeton University Press, 1971. (Originally published in 1921.)

King, K. P. *Keeping Pace with Technology: Educational Technology That Transforms.* Vol. 2: *The Challenge and Promise for Educators in Higher Education.* Cresswell, N.J.: Hampton Press, 2003.

Marsick, V. J. "Case Study." In M. W. Galbraith (ed.), *Adult Learning Methods.* (2nd ed.) Malabar, Fla.: Krieger, 1998.

Merriam, S., and Caffarella, R. *Learning in Adulthood.* (2nd ed.) San Francisco: Jossey-Bass, 1999.

Mezirow, J. *Education for Perspective Transformation: Women's Reentry Programs in Community Colleges.* New York: Center for Adult Education, Teachers College, Columbia University, 1975.

Mezirow, J. "Perspective Transformation." *Adult Education,* 1978, *28,* 100–110.

Mezirow, J. *Transformative Dimensions of Adult Learning.* San Francisco: Jossey-Bass, 1991.

Mezirow, J., and Associates. *Learning as Transformation.* San Francisco: Jossey-Bass, 2000.

Rudolph, F. *The American College and University: A History.* Athens: University of Georgia Press, 1990.

Schön, D. *Educating the Reflective Practitioner: Toward a New Design for Teaching and Learning in the Professions.* San Francisco: Jossey-Bass, 1987.

Selman, G. "The Enemies of Adult Education." *Canadian Journal of University Continuing Education,* 1989, *15,* 68–81.

Taylor, E. *The Theory and Practice of Transformative Learning: A Critical Review.* Columbus, Ohio: ERIC Clearinghouse on Adult, Career, and Vocational Education, 1998. (ED 423 422)

PATRICIA CRANTON is a professor of adult education at Saint Francis Xavier University in Nova Scotia, Canada.

KATHLEEN P. KING is an associate professor and program director of adult education and human resource development at Fordham University's Graduate School of Education in New York City.

5

The Motivational Framework for Culturally Responsive Teaching is presented as a guide to foster participation, learning, and transfer throughout a professional development program for all participants.

Fostering Motivation in Professional Development Programs

Raymond J. Wlodkowski

Increasingly, professional development programs are multicultural environments where instructors must relate their content to participants of varying backgrounds. Instruction that ignores their norms of behavior and communication provokes resistance. In contrast, engagement in learning is the visible outcome of motivation, the natural capacity to direct energy in the pursuit of a goal. Recent research in neuroscience confirms that emotions powerfully influence our motivation (Ratey, 2001). In turn, our emotions are socialized through culture—the deeply learned confluence of language, beliefs, values, and behaviors that pervades every aspect of our lives.

Professional development is an arena where emotional reactions to instruction can heighten or dampen an individual's desire to learn. For the sake of illustration, let us look at the feeling of embarrassment. Embarrassment is an emotion that usually decreases motivation to learn. However, what causes embarrassment may differ across cultures because cultures differ in their definition of an intimate situation and an appropriate response to it (Kitayama and Markus, 1994). When a teacher of adults asks them to disclose personal feelings about an incident, some people enjoy sharing such information with others who are relatively unknown to them. But studies consistently reveal that self-disclosure of this nature may be incompatible with the cultural values of Asian Americans, Latinos, and American Indians, who often reserve expression of personal feelings for the intimacy of family (Sue and Sue, 1990). A request for self-disclosure might be disconcerting for people from these ethnic backgrounds. This example

NEW DIRECTIONS FOR ADULT AND CONTINUING EDUCATION, no. 98, Summer 2003   © Wiley Periodicals, Inc.

highlights how sensitive educators and trainers have to be to the cultural backgrounds of their learners and how thoughtful they must be about the methods they use to instruct them.

The Motivational Framework for Culturally Responsive Teaching

The research-based understanding of motivation (Lambert and McCombs, 1998) is that it is part of human nature to be curious, to be active, to initiate thought and behavior, to make meaning from experience, and to be effective at what we value. These primary sources of motivation reside in all of us, across all cultures. When learners can see that what they are learning makes sense and is important, they become motivated. This view of motivation is often regarded as an *intrinsic motivation perspective* (Deci, Koestner, and Ryan, 2001). Theories of intrinsic motivation have been successfully applied and researched in areas such as cross-cultural studies and adult learning (Csikszentmihalyi and Csikszentmihalyi, 1988; Wlodkowski, 1999) and education, work, and sports (Deci and Ryan, 1985).

The Motivational Framework for Culturally Responsive Teaching respects different individual cultures and works at the same time to create a common culture in the learning situation that all adults can accept. This framework includes four motivational conditions that the instructor and the learners collaboratively create or enhance:

- *Establishing inclusion:* Creating a learning atmosphere in which learners and instructors feel respected by and connected to one another
- *Developing attitude:* Creating a favorable disposition toward the learning experience through personal relevance and choice
- *Enhancing meaning:* Creating challenging, thoughtful learning experiences that include learners' perspectives and values
- *Engendering competence:* Creating an understanding that learners are effective in learning something they value

These conditions are essential for developing intrinsic motivation among all participants in a professional development program. These motivational conditions work in concert. They occur together in the moment as well as over a period of time. Program developers need to plan to establish and coordinate the conditions.

A good place to begin is by being clear about the purpose of the program (Caffarella, 2002). Equally important is gaining an understanding of the participants (Wlodkowski, 1999). I agree with Lawler and King (2000) that professional development efforts should build on principles of adult learning and be contextual, fundamental, and responsible. In addition, their leadership strategies for credibility, institutional commitment, research, and action planning are supported by my experience in the field. These considerations are essential to creating an excellent professional development program.

Participation and Learning

Let us look at participation, learning, and transfer as a logical triangle. Unless adults participate, they cannot learn, and without learning there is no possibility for transfer—that is, to apply what they have learned to their life or workplace. Insufficient support for any of these three elements is largely responsible for the exasperated refrain "Why don't they change?" that is heard commonly among professional developers and administrators. If we begin with participation and use the motivational conditions of inclusion, attitude, and meaning from the framework as lenses for understanding and strategy, we gain guidance for the professional development process.

Adults "participate" in the professional development process when they are *engaged* in substantive actions, either individually or together, that require complex thinking to construct new skills or deeper meaning. Most participation requires adult reflection, dialogue, or practice that results in a product—whether an essay, a report, a golf swing, or a better way of teaching. From this definition we can see that participation and learning are inseparable. No matter what the prior knowledge or prerequisite skills needed may be, paying attention and being involved are critical for new learning to occur during professional development.

Establishing Inclusion. Often professional development deals with learning that is needed but not necessarily valued by a significant number of the participants. Technological innovations are a common example. Sometimes diversity efforts fall into this taxonomy, with the added challenge of being controversial. Prochaska (1999) calls this the *contemplation stage of change:* you know where you need to go but you are not quite ready yet. At times like this, strategies for establishing inclusion are very important, especially at the beginning of the program. When the program leader sets a tone that each person's perspective is welcome in a climate of respect, intrinsic motivation can emerge because people can be authentic and voice relevant matters. Creating a means for helping people to feel connected draws forth intrinsic motivation because social needs are met and they can risk the mistakes true learning involves as well as share their resources and strengths (Wlodkowski and Ginsberg, 1995). Described next are three important strategies (Wlodkowski, 1999) that enhance respect and connection.

• *Multidimensional sharing* refers to those occasions, from introduction exercises to social activities, when people have a better chance to see one another as complete and evolving human beings who have mutual needs, emotions, and experiences. These opportunities give a human face to professional development, help break down stereotypes, and support the identification of the self in the realm of another person's world. As introductory activities these are usually most inclusive and motivating when they help people learn each other's names, validate the unique experience of the individuals involved, connect to the subject matter at hand, and relieve the normal tension that most new groups feel at the beginning of a professional development program. The following is a safe and basic example that can be used as a small or large group process: each person (a) introduces herself or himself; (b) names one, and up to five, of the places he or she has lived; (c) offers one expectation, concern, or hope he or she has for the program. The range of possibilities for multidimensional sharing is enormous. The caution is to be more subtle than intrusive.

• *Collaborative learning* refers to the variety of educational approaches involving joint intellectual efforts by learners, or learners and instructors together. In these situations, participants are working in groups of two or more, mutually constructing understanding, solutions, meanings, applications, or products. Although there is wide variability in collaborative activities, most emphasize the learners' exploration and interpretation of the program material to an equal or greater extent than the instructor's explication of it. Social needs and the challenge to create something together energize the group. Brainstorming is an excellent example of an introductory way to use this strategy. To ensure supportive relationships in the group for professional development, collaborative and cooperative learning should be used throughout the program (Johnson and Johnson, 1995).

• *Participation guidelines* are appreciated when professional development is challenging, controversial, and interactive. By clearly identifying the kinds of interactions and discussion that will be encouraged and discouraged, the instructor and learners create a climate of safety, ensuring that everyone will be respected. The first meeting is an appropriate time to establish these guidelines and to request cooperation in following them. The guidelines listed here are widely used and usually acceptable (Griffin, 1997):

Listen carefully, especially to perspectives different from yours.
Keep personal information shared in the group confidential.
Speak from your own experience, saying, for example, "I think . . ." or "In my experience I have found . . . ," rather than generalizing your experience to others by saying, for example, "People say . . . ," or "We believe . . ."
Do no blaming or scapegoating.
Avoid generalizing about groups of people.
Share airtime.
Focus on your own learning.

Instructors who use participation guidelines usually have a few that are nonnegotiable (Tatum, 1992). Participation guidelines prevent and reduce feelings of fear, awkwardness, embarrassment, and shame. They also provide a safety net for critical discourse. They may be left open for further additions as the program proceeds.

Developing Attitude. The pragmatism of most adults makes *personal relevance* a key ingredient in developing a positive attitude at the outset of a professional development program. Participants are extremely sensitive to the degree to which they can identify their perspectives, needs, and values in the content and processes of the program. The program is relevant when learning reflects the personal, communal, and cultural meanings of the learners in a manner that shows a respectful awareness of their perspective. For example, two participants may both believe their company has to do something to diminish sexual harassment, the program's focus. However, what constitutes sexual harassment may be quite different for each participant. A relevant workshop will have to address both points of view respectfully.

Relevance leads to what human beings experience as interest, the emotional nutrient for a positive attitude toward learning. When we feel interested we usually have to make choices to follow that interest in the most meaningful way. That is why opportunities for adults to select what, with whom, and how to learn and be assessed can be so important in developing a positive attitude toward learning. When we teach diverse groups, we often do not know all the possible meanings, so these choices—such as how to learn (learning styles and multiple intelligences)—are usually determined in cooperation with the participants. Using the topic of sexual harassment again, one learner may prefer to analyze court decisions whereas the other may prefer to role-play a manager dealing with a complaint. Two strategies (Wlodkowski, 1999) likely to develop a positive attitude in the beginning of a professional development program follow:

• *Relevant learning models:* Whenever participants witness people similar to themselves (in age, gender, ethnicity, class, and so on) competently perform the desired professional development goal, their self-confidence is heightened, because they are prone to believe that they too possess the capability to master such activities. These people also convey information more likely to be relevant to the perspectives and values of the participants themselves. With film and video technology we have creative and economical ways to offer learners vicarious examples that are pertinent and realistic. Past participants are an excellent source for live modeling sessions. For example, the instructor of a program to develop action research methods could present a panel of past participants who have successfully conducted research to share their experiences and findings with current participants.

• *The K-W-L strategy:* Originated by Ogle (1986), this strategy is an elegant way to construct meaning for a new topic or concept based on the participants' prior knowledge. Adults have a storehouse of experiences that can give extraordinary meaning to novel ideas. During the first phase of the strategy, the participants identify what they think they know about the topic. Whether the topic is on-line learning, project management, or mentoring, this is a nonthreatening way to list some of the unique and varied ways adults understand something. It allows for multiple perspectives and numerous historical contexts. This discussion can involve drawing, storytelling, critical incidents, and predictions. In the second phase, the participants suggest what they want to know about the topic. This information may be listed as questions or subtopics for exploration and research. In the last phase, the participants identify what they have learned, which may be the answers to their questions, important related information, and perhaps new information that counters some inaccuracies they may have held prior to the program.

Enhancing Meaning. Participants create meaning as they *engage* themselves in *challenging* learning activities. In engagement, the learners are active and might be searching, evaluating, constructing, creating, or organizing some kind of learning material into new or better ideas, memories, skills, values, feelings, understandings, solutions, or decisions. Engagement is the process, and challenge is the opportunity. The challenge often has a goal-like quality and requires some degree of capacity, skill, or knowledge on the part of the learners, as in the case of solving a problem. A challenging learning experience in an engaging format about a relevant topic is intrinsically motivating because it increases the complexity of skill and knowledge about something important to the participants. Two challenging and engaging strategies (Wlodkowski, 1999) follow:

• *Posing a problem:* A problem is any situation in which a person wants to achieve a goal but an obstacle exists. This may be a condition on campus or in the workplace, such as how to make one's college or job more available to low-income people. Or it may be more specific, such as how to solve a management problem at work. The more the problem—often presented as a case study—poses a mystery, fascinates, or intrigues, the stronger participant motivation will be.

• *Creating a simulation:* Simulations are learning procedures that include role-playing, exercises, and games that allow participants to practice and apply their learning in contexts that are not genuine but are sufficiently realistic. When participants can sincerely experience perspectives, ideas, skills, and situations approximating authentic instances of life, they have a real opportunity to enhance the meaning of what they are learning as well as become more proficient. These methods are also excellent for the development of empathy and validation. They give participants the chance to take on the viewpoints and rationales of people from different backgrounds, as in the case of a role-play in which a lesbian couple and a heterosexual couple discuss the merits of a proposed policy on domestic partnerships on campus.

Engendering Competence. Although transfer is influenced by all four motivational conditions, it is most focused in the condition of competence. Competence is evidence that one is effective at what one values, and it is the raison d'être for any professional development program. Competence is usually engendered through some form of assessment that is *authentic* to the world of the participants and allows them to realize some degree of *effectiveness* with their new learning. Authentic assessment is connected to the learner's life circumstances, frames of reference, and values. For example, if a case study were used as an authentic assessment, it would require participants to respond to a situation that mirrors their work lives with the resources and conditions that are normally available. Effectiveness is the learners' awareness of how well they know or can apply what they have learned. In the example of the case study, the learners would likely want feedback about how well their responses resolve the issues presented by this case study to understand the effectiveness of those responses. A primary strategy (Wlodkowski, 1999) to develop participant confidence and ensure transfer follows:

• *Performance assessment:* Performance assessment is an evaluation task that reflects (1) the breadth, depth, and development of participant learning; (2) learning experiences connected to real-life needs of participants; and (3) participant reflection and self-monitoring. Here is where the objectives for professional development have extreme importance because they usually determine to a large extent the construction of this assessment. So if we said that as a result of a professional development program *faculty will learn instructional and communication methods that support student individual expression and foster mutual respect,* then someplace along the way we have to give the faculty a chance to do so. This may occur in response to a written case study, an enacted problem on videotape, or a scripted simulation. Also, we will need some criteria for faculty to judge their own effectiveness. This could be according to predetermined criteria, mutual consensus, expert judgment, or the suggestions of colleagues who are experienced multicultural educators. The more participants are aware of effectively learning something, the more likely they will be to use what they have learned.

With this objective, the professional development program might end with an action plan developed by each faculty member for his or her courses and publicly posted for feedback from colleagues and the instructor. Action plans work like goal-setting strategies and deepen competence and transfer. They help participants organize what they are learning and clarify how to apply it to their real-world situations. Yet much more is needed to sustain the new learning.

More About Transfer

Partly because of reciprocity and shared experience, *peer coaching* (Ginsberg and Wlodkowski, 2000), the application of new learning on campus or in the workplace, deepens proficiency in using fresh knowledge and skills. We know from studies in situated cognition (Bredo, 1994) that the context in which we learn to practice evolving skills has an enormous impact on our ability to transfer and maintain this new learning effectively. We are more likely to retain and use what we have competently applied in our own work settings.

Action research (Glanz, 1999) is another way to sustain new learning. It is a systematic and organized method of obtaining valid evidence that can be used in a work setting to inform the application of new skills or new courses of action. For example, after identifying that discipline problems should decrease as a result of consistently applying motivating teaching strategies learned in a professional development program, teachers could collect information and data to determine the extent to which such results are occurring. Reviewing these research results may help them to refine or alter their use of the teaching strategies.

Balancing pressure with support in the work setting for fledging practices learned in the professional development program sustains their proficient development. In education, research (Moffett, 2000) shows that large-scale innovations live or die by the amount and quality of assistance their practitioners receive once they are back in their schools. Usually administrators need to apply some pressure to have the new practices used. However, they must also offer organizational and personal support to help their personnel to learn and assimilate these practices further—to move from their old and more comfortable ways to their new, and often initially, more challenging ways of working.

Conclusion

We have found peer coaching, action research, and balancing pressure with support to be essential strategies for initiating successful transfer and change among educators (French, 2001; Ginsberg, 2001; Ginsberg and Wlodkowski, 2000). With the Motivational Framework for Culturally Responsive Teaching as an approach to carrying out instruction, and with greater attention to transfer, we have a means to enable *all* adults to learn well and to apply what they have learned. As educators and trainers, we are much better today at "getting it right" in the professional development program itself. Sustaining change on a long-term basis, however, remains more elusive. Now we can use our awareness of our progress as program developers to inspire us to learn more about sustaining the changes we have skillfully enhanced.

References

Bredo, E. "Reconstructing Educational Psychology: Situated Cognition and Deweyian Pragmatism." *Educational Psychologist,* 1994, 29(1), 23–35.

Caffarella, R. S. *Planning Programs for Adult Learners: A Practical Guide for Educators, Trainers, and Staff Developers.* (2nd ed.) San Francisco: Jossey-Bass, 2002.

Csikszentmihalyi, M., and Csikszentmihalyi, I. S. *Optimal Experience: Psychological Studies of Flow in Consciousness.* Cambridge: Cambridge University Press, 1988.

Deci, E. L., Koestner, R., and Ryan, R. M. "Extrinsic Rewards and Intrinsic Motivation in Education: Reconsidered Once Again." *Review of Educational Research,* 2001, 71(1), 1–28.

Deci, E. L., and Ryan, R. M. *Intrinsic Motivation and Self-Determination in Human Behavior.* New York: Plenum, 1985.

French, R. "A Tale of Four Schools." *Journal of Staff Development,* 2001, 22(2), 19–23.

Ginsberg, M. B. "By the Numbers." *Journal of Staff Development,* 2001, 22(2), 44–47.

Ginsberg, M. B., and Wlodkowski, R. J. *Creating Highly Motivating Classrooms for All Students: A Schoolwide Approach to Powerful Teaching with Diverse Learners.* San Francisco: Jossey-Bass, 2000.

Glanz, J. "Action Research." *Journal of Staff Development,* 1999, 20(3), 22–23.

Griffin, P. "Facilitating Social Justice Education Courses." In M. Adams, L. A. Bell, and P. Griffin (eds.), *Teaching for Diversity and Social Justice: A Sourcebook.* New York: Routledge, 1997.

Johnson, D. W., and Johnson, R. T. *Cooperative, Competitive, and Individualistic Procedures for Educating Adults: A Comparative Analysis.* Minneapolis: Cooperative Learning Center, University of Minnesota, 1995.

Kitayama, S., and Markus, H. R. (eds.). *Emotion and Culture: Empirical Studies of Mutual Influence.* Washington, D.C.: American Psychological Association, 1994.

Lambert, N. M., and McCombs, B. L. "Introduction to Learner-Centered Schools and Classrooms as a Direction for School Reform." In N. M. Lambert and B. L. McCombs (eds.), *How Students Learn: Reforming Schools Through Learner-Centered Education.* Washington, D.C.: American Psychological Association, 1998.

Lawler, P. A., and King, K. P. "Faculty Development: Leadership Strategies for Success." *Journal of Continuing Higher Education,* 2000, 28(2), 12–20.

Moffett, C. A. "Sustaining Change: The Answers Are Blowing in the Wind." *Educational Leadership,* 2000, 57(7), 35–38.

Ogle, D. "The K-W-L: A Teaching Model That Develops Active Reading of Expository Text." *Reading Teacher,* 1986, 39, 564–576.

Prochaska, J. "How Do People Change, and How Can We Change to Help Many More People?" In M. A. Hubble, B. L. Duncan, and S. D. Miller (eds.), *The Heart and Soul of Change: What Works in Therapy.* Washington, D.C.: American Psychological Association, 1999.

Ratey, J. J. *A User's Guide to the Brain.* New York: Pantheon, 2001.

Sue, D. W., and Sue, D. *Counseling the Culturally Different: Theory and Practice.* (2nd ed.) New York: Wiley, 1990.

Tatum, B. D. "Talking About Race, Learning About Racism: The Application of Racial Identity Development Theory in the Classroom." *Harvard Educational Review,* 1992, 62(1), 1–24.

Wlodkowski, R. J. *Enhancing Adult Motivation to Learn: A Comprehensive Guide for Teaching All Adults.* (Rev. ed.) San Francisco: Jossey-Bass, 1999.

Wlodkowski, R. J., and Ginsberg, M. B. *Diversity and Motivation: Culturally Responsive Teaching.* San Francisco: Jossey-Bass, 1995.

RAYMOND J. WLODKOWSKI is professor and director of the Center for the Study of Accelerated Learning in the School for Professional Studies at Regis University, Denver.

6

Educators of adults come to professional development in educational technology with many needs and concerns. The model presented in this chapter provides principles, insights, and strategies to meet these needs and prepare educators for lifelong learning in this challenging area.

Learning the New Technologies: Strategies for Success

Kathleen P. King

Frustration, inspiration, anticipation, anger, glee. . . . What single force is capable of stirring such varied and emotional responses? The World Series? Organizational downsizing? Election to public office? No, it is even closer to each of us and therefore more imminent and personal. Permeating every aspect of our personal and professional lives—from job searches to research, payroll to publicity, house hunting to pet screening—technology has opened up the resources of the world to those who have access to it and know how to use it.

In a short period of time, technology has become both an important vehicle and a major expense for education, business, and government (Carr, 2001; Olsen, 2001). And yet tied to this commodity are expectations, memories, and emotions that adults must confront as they seek to grab hold of the golden ring and win another ride on the revolving carousel of innovation, education, adoption, and diffusion (King, 2003). For we are all keenly aware that to lose a place on this carousel is possibly to lose our place in the future.

Educators and trainers are acutely conscious of the need to stay current with technology for many reasons. But we are all plagued by worries as we see new technologies arise and gain a hold on business and popular culture. *Will I be able to learn this technology? Will it be available at my workplace? Will it be required by my work or organization? What will my adult learners expect from me regarding this technology? Do we need to revise the way we teach because of it? Do we need to revise the curriculum? Can our current resources handle this new technology? Do we need to upgrade?* These and

NEW DIRECTIONS FOR ADULT AND CONTINUING EDUCATION, no. 98, Summer 2003 © Wiley Periodicals, Inc.

many other questions come up for educators and trainers when they hear about new technologies every day.

As educators of adults see the blur of technology innovation and adoption around them, they need to have opportunities to learn, experiment, and apply technology to their classrooms and areas of expertise (King, 2001). How do we create experiences that provide such opportunities? How do we cultivate environments where educators deluged with information and emotion can feel safe, respected, and challenged at the same time? What are the keys to creating professional development programs that encourage educators to discover new possibilities for teaching and learning through technology?

Professional development in educational technology that provides such an environment is the key to the successful future of teachers of adults. This chapter will explore their needs and risks in learning technology, and it will present principles and strategies that professional developers can use to prepare educators of adults to effectively capture the potential of technology for their learners and their classrooms.

High Visibility, High Risk

As technology is assimilated into so many aspects of our lives and work, there rises an urgent cry for it to be adopted in educational settings too. Currently, technology has high visibility in our global economies and world. Increasingly, people rely on it to deliver information, goods, entertainment, and education to them. Businesses rely on it for communications across the office and around the world. Business documents are shared in universal formats, and projections are made through complex algorithms that have become accessible through improved technologies. All this dependence on technology comes at a high price—high visibility and high risk.

As technology's visibility has increased, so have the stakes. In more and more cases computer viruses and worms cripple productivity, such as when the Code Red worm brought Internet servers to a grinding halt as it infected computer software and overwhelmed communication channels with bogus e-mails (Lemos, 2001). On-line learning, news services, and research sites were among those hit and disabled in this daylong siege, and the problems later resurfaced repeatedly for several months. Costs to business included the hours spent trying to access and use resources and the additional technical support staff and technicians hired to correct the problems. A still more acute demonstration of the susceptibility of our society's technology dependency happened on September 11, 2001, when the terrorist strikes in New York, Pennsylvania, and Washington, D.C., illustrated the vulnerability of our technological infrastructure. In New York City, some companies tragically lost their employees and their infrastructure; others not physically damaged by the attacks were crippled for weeks as major telecommunications trunk lines were disabled, resulting in jammed phone, fax, and

Internet access. In Washington, D.C., some government services halted or delayed their mail deliveries for months. As our communities and businesses increasingly rely on technology, we experience events beyond human control; organizations have to determine how to cope with the consequences of disrupted services, including communication (University of California at Davis, 2001).

From another perspective, the technology emphasis in our communities and businesses also feeds the need for equipping persons of all ages to use technology in their various capacities as students, employees, and private citizens. Organizations are vulnerable to the competition if their services are not accessible and user-friendly through technology. Such risks are faced day after day in our boardrooms, be they in corporations, educational institutions, nonprofit organizations, or government (Carlson, 2001). Organizational leaders and members alike need to make innumerable technology-related decisions daily.

In such an environment, professional development in technology becomes an urgent concern for organizations and individuals. Although there is the risk of financial loss and obsolescence for organizations that fail to adopt and upgrade technology swiftly, the losses to individuals who fail to adopt and learn technology can also be dire, affecting their financial welfare, education, and relationships. Adults need to constantly cope with new software applications and versions, new hardware, and new processing paths for communications and production. Just as organizations face great financial demand in keeping pace with technology innovation, individuals also stand at the edge of risk every time they need to master new technologies. Against this backdrop of urgency, necessity, and demand, how we provide technology training can determine individuals' success in many facets of their lives. Although the highly charged climate for organizations facing new technologies is often noted, the threat and risk for individuals is not addressed often enough. Unlike organizational mandates to integrate technology, making the learning process seem a threat or mere drudgery, professional development that helps individuals gain confidence and be successful can produce rewards for both individuals and organizations.

Understanding the Needs and Risks of Educators of Adults

As we look at educators of adults and what is expected of them, we see that they have eight needs and distinctive demands for their learning technology. First, educators of adults are, by the nature of their varied work responsibilities, usually managing overloaded schedules. Between curriculum development, lesson preparation, student assistance, staff meetings, and committee service, their days are already brimming with demands that pull them in many directions at once (Alstete, 2000; Lawler and King, 2000). Given these conditions, professional developers need to streamline learning experiences so that they deliver essential topics and materials in readily accessible formats.

Second, educators may be embarrassed or may regret that they are not current in technology applications. Others may be confused as they listen to their own learners and to their colleagues. Thus, educators need to face the challenges of learning technology in an environment where they feel safe and respected (King, 2003).

Third, educators of adults are used to being the experts in their fields. As new technology confronts them, they are placed in the role of learners in a field for which they may have little aptitude. Professional development challenges their identification as experts and casts them in a public and perhaps unfamiliar role as learners. Recommendations for such professional development thus include continually cultivating a climate of respect for these educators, building a scaffold of learning that is based on their strengths, and guiding them in considering what it means to be lifelong learners. All of these approaches support, reassure, and strengthen educators as they venture into the constantly changing realm of technology.

The fourth need of educators in learning technology is universal—like everyone, they must learn it constantly. If they help build these teachers' identity as lifelong learners, professional developers can provide multiple skills and strategies to aid them in continuing their learning beyond formal settings. A vision of lifelong learning as an opportunity for refreshment can encourage positive expectations rather than make learning just seem endless (King, 2003).

Fifth, just as experts in academia may not have a background in education courses, most educators of adults have had little preparation in integrating technology into teaching and learning. Experience has shown that when they gain firsthand experience with technology-integrated learning, educators become very excited about the possibilities for their classrooms (King, 2003). When they are given professional development experiences that engage them in discovering educational technology, the stage is set for them to consider principles of instructional design and practice.

Sixth, educators of adults urgently need assistance in integrating technology into their curricula (King, 2001). A fundamental requisite for this task is seeing themselves as a bridge between their areas of expertise and technology (King, 2003). As educators learn about technology and educational technology, they become the most effective bridge to incorporate it in their curriculum. Technology learning can open new avenues of learning, perceiving, and problem solving in all disciplines (Brown, 2000, 2001). Professional development needs to communicate these possibilities and help participants see themselves as proactive, self-directed educators. Programs in which educators create curriculum materials and gain assistance from instructional technology specialists can lay the foundation for self-directed instructional design in the future.

The seventh need emerges from a model of professional development that ties cooperative learning and application to practice. This orientation provides fertile ground for developing a community of practice (Wenger, 1998). When professional development fosters learning communities among educators, it can achieve a greater impact than when learning is confined to formal, isolated training sessions. Using cooperative learning methods in professional development sessions and introducing techniques for continuing communication lay the foundation for educators to see themselves as a community reaching for teaching excellence. As educators discuss how to use technology in their work, they discover new perspectives and points of application. The work of communities of practice will extend much further than isolated professional development initiatives.

At this point it becomes evident that professional development of educators in technology must address a wide range of needs. And while one can see similarities, it is also imperative that we recognize individuality, the eighth need. Educators approach learning technology with their own individual learning styles, content area knowledge, teaching settings, and teaching styles. Professional development that effectively empowers teaching through technology will take these differences into consideration. Technology learning that has a real impact on teaching and learning does not happen in a moment; it is the product of a common vision and a set of experiences that prepare educators to embark on a journey of learning. As educators discover their needs, face the risks, and work with professional developers who recognize the possibilities of technology learning for the classroom, they often find they are beginning a *journey of transformation* (King, 2003).

Educational Technology Professional Development as a Transformative Journey

Based on research among educators learning educational technology in specific professional development formats, I have identified this journey of transformation. This conceptualization is based on the literature and research on adult education program planning and adult learning. The journey uniquely frames the experience of learning technology to help us understand how educators go through the process to use technology and incorporate it in their teaching practice. The journey casts a kind of vision of educational technology learning as a series of transformative experiences (King, 1999, 2003). Based on data gathered from over 255 educators, this journey depicts the transformation of many educators from inexperienced, hesitant, and sometimes fearful technology users to people who can independently learn technology and discover new ways to change their teaching and learning through the medium. These stages are also consistent with our understanding of the needs of educators of adults.

As educators learn technology, research has demonstrated that they go through four stages: (1) fear and uncertainty, (2) testing and exploring, (3) affirming and connecting current knowledge, and finally, (4) a new perspective of the impact of using technology in educational processes. In the first stage, they experience uncertainty, confusion, and sometimes embarrassment as they struggle with new technologies. Often their first professional development session will be dominated by these emotions; the successful professional developer will find a way to build a safe and nurturing climate so that the educators can begin to relax and sort out introductory activities. Taking a hands-on approach, these sessions should guide the educators into activities in which they will succeed immediately. A series of brief, successful technology-based exercises bolsters confidence. In the second stage of the journey, educators use this newfound confidence to begin testing and exploring technology. Fondly referred to as the "poking stage," technology users reach beyond the predefined steps of use to try new program functions and to consider new applications to teaching and learning.

In the affirming and connecting stage, educators continue to make new connections between technology and its application to teaching and learning. They actively connect their learning with the potential for their learners. They seek out ways to incorporate what they are learning into their practice. Customarily, excitement builds rapidly at this stage, and educators begin to gain momentum and vision. The fourth stage is where they gain new perspectives. Their growing vision extends to new perspectives of teaching, incorporating new teaching strategies, and teaching content through technological means. In other words, they gain a new paradigm of education and technology, rather than viewing technology simply as a tool to support or integrate into their teaching. They begin to awaken to the possibilities of technology for fundamentally transforming their objectives for their learners and content. By using technology, new futures open for their discipline and their work—they become the makers of new knowledge and their future.

To understand the journey of transformation, we need to understand several key points. First, there is no "perfect" or expected timetable for this journey. Some adults move through some stages more quickly than others; comfort level, interest, technology access, and time are important determinants of any individual's time line. Furthermore, the journey of transformation concept is meant to provide insight into educators' learning and development; it is not meant to confine anyone to predetermined outcomes. The intent is to provide a new vision of the possibilities technology has for educators and for teaching and learning. Finally, the journey is open-ended: no one has written the final word about what educators who have experienced this transformation will accomplish. The model is an open-ended, upward spiral of learning and innovation. The worldwide community of educators of adults will chart their own courses for educational technology application.

Cultivating the Journey

Fundamental to the journey of transformation is the means to cultivate that experience. This section will briefly review the principles for professional development that can transform and then provide some specific strategies that illustrate the application of these principles.

Principles. When professional developers understand the needs, the context, and the potential of educators as adult learners, they can begin to explore the potential for their transformation and the resulting transformation of their practice of teaching and learning. This understanding is central to the journey. If we build on the principles of adult learning presented in Chapter Two of this volume as they apply to technology learning discussed in this chapter, it provides a sound basis for cultivating educators' learning and vision. Research (King, 2001, 2003) has demonstrated that learning relationships are vitally important to educators learning technology. This finding supports developers' building nurturing dialogues with educators and extending these dialogues to their greater community of practice inside the organization.

In addition, research among professional development participants indicates that active learning is fundamental to professional development that transforms. Engaging educators in hands-on applications reminds them of the learner's perspective and helps them explore different learning methods. Also, through their learning and dialogue with colleagues they can reacquaint themselves with the reality of different learning styles and needs. Building on the use of multiple active learning methods, educators can transfer their experience to practice. Planning tools are a powerful means to promote technology learning; they help educators assess their current status and needs for technology learning (pre- and post- checklists) and their learning styles (King, 2003). Multiple teaching methods should be combined to demonstrate a broad display of the potential of technology.

The final principle to cultivate the journey is follow-up. Encapsulating all of the previous principles, a perspective of learning for a lifetime will enable educators to use professional development continually. As they recognize themselves as lifelong learners they will need skills and resources to sustain them. Professional development activities can incorporate these skills in introducing new teaching and learning methods and helping educators to understand the self as learner (King, 2003). A community of learners inside and outside an organization is a powerful resource for ongoing learning, and technology can provide some of the means to support such exchange: e-mail, listservs, and Web boards, for example, which are some of the same tools that are used in distance learning (Palloff and Pratt, 1999; Porter, 1997). Professional developers should also help educators develop resources that they can use and share in their application of technology—FAQs, on-line tutorials or help sheets, and so on (Gilbert, 2001; King, 2003). If they have access to local and remote assistance, information, and communication, it will provide another essential for continued learning. These principles of adult learning, learning relationships, multiple learning activities, and follow-up briefly summarize the essentials of professional development that can transform through technology learning.

Strategies. As we consider the principles that support professional development in technology, we can gain further understanding by applying them. Here are three brief examples of such strategies:

- *Help educators appreciate and assess their current knowledge and needs in order to determine a plan of study.* Using both assessment tools and a menu of available learning activities can build confidence, expertise, skills, and a plan of action.
- *Engage educators in developing needed curricular materials rather than prototypes.* If developers go beyond skill acquisition and address teaching needs to have educators prepare materials they can actually use, it will capture their interest and commitment.
- *Reflect on practice and dialogue individually and with peers.* The synergistic potential of this strategy will encourage communities of learners to continue to seek learning opportunities, applications, and resources (King, 2003).

When the journey of transformation model is used and the principles outlined here are applied, these strategies provide a base on which developers can build additional and specific directions for empowering educators of adults through educational technology learning.

Conclusion

When organizations and professional developers begin to recognize the need to learn technology as an opportunity to transform teaching and learning, they open up new possibilities for their organizations. Informed professional developers can understand the urgent need of educators of adults to learn technology and can craft programs that will address their needs, build lifelong learning skills and communities of learners, and potentially transform both these individuals and their learning. This chapter has examined the need for continuing professional development in technology and described a model of the journey of transformation that provides principles and strategies for professional development in technology among educators of adults.

References

Alstete, J. "Post-Tenure Faculty Development: Building a System of Faculty Improvement and Appreciation." *ASHE ERIC Higher Education Report,* 2000, 27(4).

Brown, D. G. (ed.). *Teaching with Technology: Seventy-Five Professors from Eight Universities Tell Their Stories.* Bolton, Mass.: Anker, 2000.

Brown, D. G. "Teaching Strategies and Faculty Workshops." *Syllabus*, 2001, *15*(2), 22.
Carlson, S. "A Small College's Mixed Results with Technology." *Chronicle of Higher Education*, Mar. 16, 2001, p. A35.
Carr, S. "Is Anyone Making Money on Distance Education?" *Chronicle of Higher Education*, Feb. 16, 2001, p. A41.
Gilbert, S. "Staying Afloat: Open Source Professional Development." *Syllabus*, 2001, *15*(2), 24.
King, K. P. "Unleashing Technology in the Classroom: What Adult Basic Education Teachers and Organizations Need to Know." *Adult Basic Education: An Interdisciplinary Journal for Adult Literacy Educators*, 1999, *9*(3), 162–175.
King, K. P. "Professors' Transforming Perspectives of Teaching and Learning While Learning Technology." *Journal of Staff, Professional, and Organizational Development*, 2001, *18*(1), 25–32.
King, K. P. *Keeping Pace with Technology: Educational Technology That Transforms*. Vol. 2: *The Challenge and Promise for Higher Education Faculty*. Cresskill, N.J.: Hampton Press, 2003.
Lawler, P. A., and King, K. P. *Planning for Effective Faculty Development: Using Adult Learning Strategies*. Malabar, Fla.: Krieger, 2000.
Lemos, R. "Worm Has Servers Seeing 'Code Red.'" *ZDNet News*, July 19, 2001. [http://www.zdnet.com/zdhelp/stories/main/0,5594,5094345,00.html].
Olsen, F. "Eight Community Colleges Collaborate to Lower Information-Technology Expenses." *Chronicle of Higher Education*, July 27, 2001, p. A29.
Palloff, R. M., and Pratt, K. *Building Learning Communities in Cyberspace: Effective Strategies for the Online Classroom*. San Francisco: Jossey-Bass, 1999.
Porter, L. R. *Creating the Virtual Classroom: Distance Learning with the Internet*. New York: Wiley, 1997.
University of California at Davis. *Response, from a Human Resources Perspective, to Electric Power Rolling Blackout Collective Bargaining Agreements/Policy Issues*, 2001. [http://hr.ucdavis.edu/elr/blackouthrfaq.htm].
Wenger, E. *Communities of Practice: Learning, Meaning, and Identity*. Cambridge: Cambridge University Press, 1998.

KATHLEEN P. KING is an associate professor and program director of adult education and human resource development at Fordham University's Graduate School of Education in New York City.

7

This chapter looks at the challenges that higher education faculty are facing and explains how development activities that recognize faculty as adult learners in a learning organization can provide a more successful educational experience for both them and their students.

Professional Development in Higher Education

Vera C. Brancato

Higher education has been facing numerous challenges, and as a result there is a sense of unpredictability and uncertainty among educators. Societal demands, organizational demands, and student demands pressure institutions to find ways to improve the quality and effectiveness of their instruction. External demands on institutions and faculty members, coupled with internal pressures from students and the organization itself, greatly affect educators' satisfaction, vitality, and quality of life (Atkins, Brinko, Butts, Claxton, and Hubbard, 2001). Patrick and Fletcher (1998) note that faculty developers are ideally suited to assist faculty in transforming their previous notions about teaching and in confronting these challenges. Confronting these challenges requires that faculty reflect on their current practice and improve their knowledge and skills so that student learning will be enhanced (Smith, 1998). This chapter will discuss these demands and then look at the role of faculty development in the context of a learning organization.

Societal Trends and Demands

Higher education is transforming itself in an effort to meet the multiple demands that society has imposed on it. Educators, therefore, are being urged to help invent the future rather than merely transmit knowledge that will only replicate the past (Smith, 1998). This has spawned shifts in focus from teaching to learning and from operating in one specific learning environment to operating in a more global environment (Patrick and Fletcher, 1998). The explosion in information technology has created and continues to create an abundance of resources and techniques that, if properly

NEW DIRECTIONS FOR ADULT AND CONTINUING EDUCATION, no. 98, Summer 2003   © Wiley Periodicals, Inc.

incorporated into a teaching program, can inspire innovative approaches to both "teaching" and "learning" (Svinicki, 1998). Thus, faculty development has the enormous task of providing relevant learning opportunities to assist faculty in accessing and linking the world to the classroom as they become more student-focused (Marchese, 1998).

Organizational Trends and Demands

Because teaching practices and faculty roles are embedded in the university's culture, educators are redefining themselves as they try to fulfill their own professional mission and that of the organization. Rather than merely transmitting information to students, educators now have a broader sense of accountability for student learning outcomes (Fulton and Licklider, 1998). Linking faculty responsibilities more closely to the organization's aims means that faculty have become invested in meeting the organization's challenges. Efficiency, productivity, and accountability are key demands on universities as they struggle to keep tuition costs reasonable. With the intense competition among numerous providers of education, a new hierarchy of quality and effectiveness will arise. Educators need to grapple with these trends and engage in professional development activities that promote among them a renewed sense of accountability, innovation, and connection to the organization's mission and goals while also promoting professional and personal growth (Atkins, Brinko, Butts, Claxton, and Hubbard, 2001).

Student Trends and Demands

Including diverse student populations and ensuring their success are great challenges for higher education, which needs to provide an effective and supportive learning environment (Anderson, 1997). Currently, there is a large gap between educators' expectations of their students and students' own expectations for success (McGuire and Williams, 2002). More experienced, older students are entering higher education, and they are more sophisticated consumers of education. Their learning style preferences and other diverse characteristics challenge educators to employ more diverse and interactive teaching strategies in order to meet their unique needs. Students, especially nontraditional students, are increasingly demanding that education be more relevant to their personal lives and professional goals. They want to know what value has been added to their lives as a direct result of their educational experiences. They demand to be involved rather than passive recipients of factual knowledge. Thus, students rather than institutions may devise the future agenda for higher education (Levine, 2000). Noting this, faculty development initiatives need to help faculty become more comfortable with diverse needs and desires of students while at the same time teaching them about different ways to make instruction more inclusive (Anderson, 1997).

The Educator's Role and New Demands

The educator's role is to devise learning opportunities that strategically develop the skills students will need to function successfully in the work world (Lindeman, 2000). However, various constraints and pressures placed on educators can limit their ability to accomplish this task (Austin, Brocato, and Rohrer, 1997). In addition, educators are often ill-prepared to teach; they identify more with their disciplinary interest and less with teaching practice (Bakutes, 1998; Bowen and Schuster, 1986; Cranton, 1994). Confronted by diverse student needs and expectations, educators must continuously learn in order to keep up-to-date with current trends and demands (McGuire and Williams, 2002). Effective teaching is a crucial aspect of the educator's role and it draws on ongoing professional development to keep faculty vital, productive, and working together as a community of learners (Atkins, Brinko, Butts, Claxton, and Hubbard, 2001; Lunde and Wilhite, 1996).

But teaching to a high level of learning is often a struggle, because educators are frequently not knowledgeable about a variety of teaching strategies (Smith and Geis, 1996). In conjunction with this lack of adequate preparation in education, educators play multiple roles—teaching, research, and service—that pull at the little time they have to invest in their own learning (Davis, 1993). Furthermore, collaboration among colleagues in the classroom and around teaching practices is hindered by professional autonomy and classroom isolation.

Faculty who strive to discover their own capacities and potential broaden their knowledge of themselves as professionals and become more enthusiastic about their teaching. In turn, their enthusiasm and vitality can foster student excitement about learning and rekindle "the lost vision of the college or university as a community of scholars" (Katz and Henry, 1993, p. 164).

Importance of Faculty Development Initiatives

As higher education strives to face these many challenges, faculty members are finding it increasingly difficult to keep abreast not just of discipline-specific knowledge but also of teaching innovations (Heppner and Johnson, 1994). As more institutions place a higher priority on student learning, they have begun to emphasize the professional development needs of the faculty (Gillepsie, Hilsen, and Wadsworth, 2002). Thus, development programs have been initiated to help faculty reflect on their teaching and make stronger connections between teaching strategies and their disciplinary knowledge and skill (Maxwell and Kazlauskas, 1992).

Faculty development initiatives that are strategically planned, implemented, and sustainable over time encourage a perspective on teaching as a lifelong endeavor and necessitate continuous learning by faculty.

Furthermore, while learning more about their own teaching, faculty gain insight into their students' learning needs (Fulton and Licklider, 1998). In other words, faculty development should treat faculty as adult learners and employ adult learning strategies to foster their development (Lawler and King, 2000). "New visions of professional development suggest that the practices needed to support faculty learning are analogous to those needed to support student learning" (Fulton and Licklider, 1998, p. 55). Thus, in order to make connections to their teaching, faculty as adult learners should be provided with opportunities to learn about students, curriculum, and teaching strategies as they apply discipline-specific content.

Faculty Development in the Context of the Learning Organization

Faculty development that connects faculty more closely to the basic aims of the institution can help transform institutions of higher education into learning organizations (Cox, 2001). Senge (1990) describes the learning organization as one that more closely links its members to its broader mission, goals, and challenges. He identifies five components of a learning organization: *personal mastery, team learning, mental models, shared vision,* and *systems thinking.* These facilitate connections that can help the organization meet demands and challenges during times of change. Senge identifies a learning organization as a "place where people are continually discovering how they create their reality. And how they can change it" (1990, p. 13). Faculty development efforts in such a framework can help higher education thrive amid unprecedented internal and external pressures to change. Therefore, the aim of faculty development should be to strategically plan activities that employ the five components of a learning organization.

Personal Mastery. Personal mastery means being committed to lifelong learning in order to develop a special level of proficiency and skill in one's discipline (Senge, 1990). To develop proficiency and skill, faculty need to feel secure while they participate in a new learning activity. This allows for experimentation and application. Because development programs may include faculty at different moments in their professional lives, a variety of activities must be offered to meet the diverse needs at every skill level, from novice to expert (Patrick and Fletcher, 1998).

For example, workshops or small groups can encourage sharing experiences and can address specific well-defined needs of participants (Carroll, 1993). Opportunities to reflect critically on the activity and to reexamine their own goals and values are essential for educators to transfer ideas they have learned to their classroom activities. A set of structured activities that allow educators to role-play or suggest ways in which they can use the ideas presented can provide practical application to various teaching situations.

Team Learning. Collaborative endeavors for team learning include peer coaching, using master teachers as mentors, collaborative or team teaching, and videotaping teaching sessions to provide feedback on teaching performance (Seldin and Associates, 1995). In peer coaching, two or more colleagues work together to inquire and reflect on current and future skill development. By sharing ideas, they actively help teach each other, which can enhance collegiality and feedback. Educators historically have taught in isolation, but this methodology provides much-needed peer interaction and support (St. Clair, 1994). Reading and study groups also encourage discussion, debate, and sharing of ideas.

Mentoring by master professors who serve in an advisory capacity for new faculty can increase their awareness of their strengths and weaknesses (Cranton, 1994). Over time, discussions with a mentor can lead to use of new approaches and critical appraisal of one's own mastery of teaching. Team teaching is a strategy that involves shared lessons and teaching time that can help bring different talents and knowledge to the classroom. These strategies encourage collaboration and trust and serve as a vehicle for connectedness (Patrick and Fletcher, 1998).

Mental Models. As educators grow in their careers, they may begin to engage in critical analysis of their practice. This development may entail a redefinition of their mental models—or deeply ingrained assumptions and beliefs—about teaching and learning. Educators need time to reexamine their teaching practices and the underlying assumptions in order to strive for deeper learning, adapt their teaching to new findings, ideas, and techniques, and develop greater competency as teachers. Thus, activities that provide opportunities for discussion, reflection, and connection of learning at a personal level become even more critical to support the institution's mission and goals (Patrick and Fletcher, 1998).

Shared Vision. Building a shared vision involves collaboration in creating organizational goals, mission, identity, and vision (Patrick and Fletcher, 1998). Each individual's contributions become integral to the success of the organization. Rather than keeping a departmental or disciplinary focus, faculty development can strive to build collaboration and teamwork so that learning becomes a goal for each member. In addition, publishing a composite schedule of professional development activities, an index of resources and services to support professional development, and a newsletter that highlights faculty development activities can lead to greater campus awareness of upcoming development events.

Systems Thinking. Systems thinking allows us to see ourselves as connected to the outside world and envision how we can act to solve our problems and allay our concerns (Senge, 1990). Faculty development is not merely the sum of its parts; it is the system in its entirety. In a learning organization, educators and students are seen as partners in the learning process who actively become an important resource for future societal initiatives and endeavors (Bowen and Schuster, 1986). The classroom setting must allow faculty to take risks and try out new strategies (Robles, 1998). Evaluation of outcomes should be built into the process so that there is a feedback loop, allowing new strategies to be developed and previous programs to be altered based on evaluation data. Thus, faculty development should be flexible to meet the needs of individual educators and individual situations (Nelsen and Siegel, 1980).

Conclusion

Increased attention is being given to faculty development programs that address today's demands on higher education. Faculty members are being encouraged to transform their roles and responsibilities in order to enhance their teaching and student learning, and faculty development initiatives can offer them strategies for a successful transition. When faculty development recognizes that faculty members are adult learners, a more effective approach and more successful outcomes will be the result. Using the framework of the learning organization to approach these activities reinforces lifelong learning for faculty and increases the likelihood of successful educational experiences for their students.

References

Anderson, J. "Faculty Development and the Inclusion of Diversity in the College Classroom: Pedagogical and Curricular Transformation." In D. DeZure (ed.), *To Improve the Academy* (Vol. 19). Stillwater, Okla.: New Forums Press, 1997.

Atkins, S., Brinko, K., Butts, J., Claxton, C., and Hubbard, G. "Faculty Quality of Life." In D. Lieberman and C. Wehlburg (eds.), *To Improve the Academy* (Vol. 19, pp. 323–345). Bolton, Mass.: Anker, 2001.

Austin, A., Brocato, J., and Rohrer, J. "Institutional Missions, Multiple Faculty Roles: Implications for Faculty Development." In D. DeZure (ed.), *To Improve the Academy* (Vol. 16). Stillwater, Okla.: New Forums Press, 1997.

Bakutes, A. "An Examination of Faculty Development Centers." *Contemporary Education*, 1998, 69(3), 168–171.

Bowen, H., and Schuster, J. *American Professors: A National Resource Imperiled*. New York: Oxford University Press, 1986.

Carroll, R. "Implications of Adult Education Theories for Medical School Faculty Development Programs." *Medical Teacher*, 1993, 15(2–3), 163–170.

Cox, M. "Faculty Learning Communities: Change Agents for Transforming Institutions into Learning Organizations." In D. Lieberman and C. Wehlburg (eds.), *To Improve the Academy* (Vol. 19). Bolton, Mass.: Anker, 2001.

Cranton, P. "Self-Directed and Transformative Instructional Development." *Journal of Higher Education*, 1994, 65(6), 726–744.

Davis, J. *Better Teaching, More Learning: Strategies for Success in Postsecondary Settings*. Phoenix, Ariz.: American Council on Education and Oryx Press, 1993.

Fulton, C., and Licklider, B. "Supporting Faculty Development in an Era of Change." In M. Kaplan (ed.), *To Improve the Academy* (Vol. 17). Stillwater, Okla.: New Forums Press, 1998.

Gillepsie, K., Hilsen, L., and Wadsworth, E. *A Guide to Faculty Development: Practical Advice, Examples, and Resources*. Bolton, Mass.: Anker, 2002.

Heppner, P., and Johnson, J. "New Horizons in Counseling: Faculty Development." *Journal of Counseling and Development*, 1994, 72(5), 451–453.

Katz, J., and Henry, M. *Turning Professors into Teachers: A New Approach to Faculty Development and Student Learning.* Phoenix, Ariz.: American Council on Education and Oryx Press, 1993.

Lawler, P., and King, K. *Planning for Effective Faculty Development: Using Adult Learning Strategies.* Malabar, Fla.: Krieger, 2000.

Levine, A. "The Future of Colleges: Nine Inevitable Changes." *Chronicle of Higher Education,* Oct. 27, 2000, pp. B10–B11.

Lindeman, C. "The Future of Nursing Education." *Journal of Nursing Education,* 2000, *39*(1), 5–12.

Lunde, J., and Wilhite, M. "Innovative Teaching and Teaching Improvement." In L. Richlin (ed.), *To Improve the Academy* (Vol. 15). Stillwater, Okla.: New Forums Press, 1996.

Marchese, T. "Not-So-Distant Competitors: How New Providers Are Remaking the Postsecondary Marketplace." *AAHE Bulletin,* 1998, *50*(9), 3–11.

Maxwell, W., and Kazlauskas, E. "Which Faculty Development Methods Really Work in Community Colleges? A Review of Research." *Community/Junior College Quarterly,* 1992, *16*, 351–360.

McGuire, S., and Williams, D. "The Millennial Learner: Challenges and Opportunities." In D. Lieberman and C. Wehlburg (eds.), *To Improve the Academy* (Vol. 20). Bolton, Mass.: Anker, 2002.

Nelsen, W., and Siegel, M. (eds.). *Effective Approaches to Faculty Development.* Washington, D.C.: Association of American Colleges, 1980.

Patrick, S., and Fletcher, J. "Faculty Developers as Change Agents: Transforming Colleges and Universities into Learning Organizations." In M. Kaplan (ed.), *To Improve the Academy* (Vol. 17). Stillwater, Okla.: New Forums Press, 1998.

Robles, H. *Andragogy, the Adult Learner, and Faculty as Learners.* East Lansing, Mich.: National Center for Research on Teacher Learning, 1998. (ED 426 740)

Seldin, P., and Associates. *Improving College Teaching.* Bolton, Mass.: Anker, 1995.

Senge, P. *The Fifth Discipline: The Art and Practice of the Learning Organization.* New York: Doubleday, 1990.

Smith, B. "Adopting a Strategic Approach to Managing Change in Learning and Teaching." In M. Kaplan (ed.), *To Improve the Academy* (Vol. 17). Stillwater, Okla.: New Forums Press, 1998.

Smith, R., and Geis, G. "Professors as Clients for Instructional Development." In L. Richlin (ed.), *To Improve the Academy* (Vol. 15). Stillwater, Okla.: New Forums Press, 1996.

St. Clair, K. "Faculty-to-Faculty Mentoring in the Community College: An Instructional Component of Faculty Development." *Community College Review,* 1994, *22*(3), 23–35.

Svinicki, M. "Divining the Future for Faculty Development: Five Hopeful Signs and One Caveat." In M. Kaplan (ed.), *To Improve the Academy* (Vol. 17). Stillwater, Okla.: New Forums Press, 1998.

VERA C. BRANCATO is director of the Center for the Enhancement of Teaching and associate professor of nursing at Kutztown University of Pennsylvania.

8

A regional director of a staff development consortium provides his perspective on current adult basic education practice.

Professional Development in Adult Basic Education

Georges Marceau

According to a recent National Center for the Study of Adult Learning and Literacy (NCSALL) staff development study (2001), adult educators state a need to have access to colleagues and program directors in order to exchange ideas and get feedback on their teaching. They seek an environment that fosters "an ethic of collaboration," encouraging experienced teachers to work with and support newer colleagues. Educators also want a connection to larger statewide initiatives. They want national organizations that provide resources such as journals and Internet learning opportunities and that appreciate learning of current trends and information on the field of adult education (Smith, Hofer, and Gillespie, 2001). This chapter explores professional development of adult basic education instructors by reviewing their background, providing examples of professional development initiatives, and offering recommendations for future practice.

Who Are Adult Educators?

Adult basic education instructors are a hardy, dedicated lot. They work in a variety of settings—from volunteer tutoring in libraries, to migrant family education on farms, to classroom-based high school diploma preparation programs. They instruct an even wider variety of adult students in terms of age, educational experience, and learning needs. But these educators are bound together by serving the needs of adults in basic skills in ESOL, GED preparation, literacy, community and continuing education, and adult basic education. Many adult educators are part-time workers because there is minimal funding for programs. Others are full-time instructors in school districts or community-based organizations. Instruction takes place from a distance, one-on-one, or in traditional classroom settings. Outreach educators and others who work in nonadult education sites often feel isolated and want to collaborate with other adult basic education instructors.

Despite this adversity, a characteristic shared by all adult educators is their enjoyment in providing basic skills instruction to other adults. They thrive on the immediate feedback that learners give them and the learners' excitement as they acquire and apply new knowledge in family, work, and civic and societal participation. Indeed, their value as educators and the significant contribution they make to American society are often only recognized by the learners themselves. When they help their students succeed educationally and vicariously experience that success, it gives these adult educators the thrill of teaching, reconfirming their original calling to the profession. This rewarding experience attracts many professionals from other fields to work with adults in their literacy, vocational, and personal achievement endeavors.

Adult educators come from many sectors—some were previously teachers in the K–12 system, others worked in business and industry—and often they took a circuitous route to their current practice. Many of these adult educators do not have formal preparation in teaching their content area to adults but have acquired experience and expertise through on-the-job training, mentoring, self-study, and staff development.

Because of their diversity in professional preparation and educational background, the field requires consistent and constant delivery of professional development services (Kutner and Tibbetts, 1997). Consistent professional development provides a sense of belonging; it recognizes and validates the educators' skills and dedication (Tolbert, 2001). From this recognition comes a willingness among educators to improve their practice and apply new learning and techniques with their adult learners. For those who have made a career change into adult education, the validation and cohesiveness of a supportive and active profession are extremely beneficial. Effective professional development systems are tied to state and federal reform initiatives, include other local and statewide activities and services, and are based on "systemically determined needs of both instructors and programs" (Kutner and Tibbetts, 1997, p. 1).

Federal Legislation on Funding for Professional Development

In order for delivery of professional development for adult educators to be high-quality, it needs to be systematic and organized. Funding to states for leadership activities for practitioners began with the Adult Education Act of 1978, when states were required to set aside 10 percent of their federal adult education grant funding for professional development. Then in 1991 the National Literacy Act (NLA) required states to allocate 15 percent of their federal funds to professional development. This has continued under the Workforce Investment Act, Title 2, Adult and Family Literacy Act, passed by Congress in 1998; however, states are now allowed to spend a maximum of 12.5 percent of their federal adult education grant funds on professional development. Federal funds targeted for state leadership activities that include technical assistance, program evaluation, and curriculum development decreased from $14 million in 2001 to $9.5 million in 2002 and are expected to remain at this level for fiscal year 2003 (National Institute for Literacy, 2002). The systems that states have set up to deliver these programs have varied, from centralized to locally organized structures, employing both experienced staff developers and local practitioners. Delivery itself is equally varied—mentoring, conferences, workshops, on-line and teleconference media, and action research are all used.

Federally Funded Support and Resources Available to the Field

The National Institute for Literacy (NIFL), a federal agency dedicated to building national, regional, and state literacy infrastructures, is an outcome of the NLA. Among the projects that NIFL has supported are Bridges to Practice, a comprehensive research-based initiative that provides information about serving adults with learning disabilities, and Equipped for the Future (EFF), a standards-based system that aims to improve the quality, outcomes, and accountability of adult education and family literacy programs and systems in the United States. Recognizing the need to make information and the exchange of ideas accessible through technology, NIFL created the LINCS system, an Internet-based information resource and communication system that provides discussion and information exchanges among researchers and practitioners, connecting local, statewide, and national efforts in the field of adult education. The Web site (http://www.nifl.gov) is well-known among practitioners seeking information on and connection to their work in the field. Pro-Net (http://www.pro-net2000.org) is another resource available to adult education professionals; it is a federally funded project that provides infrastructures to support professional development, including guides and "train-the-trainer" modules, national and regional conferences, and Web site resources.

NCSALL, another project, is a collaboration between the Harvard Graduate School of Education and World Education; its mission is to "conduct the research, development, evaluation, and dissemination needed to build effective, cost-efficient adult learning and literacy programs" (2001, p. 2). The organization publishes *Focus on Basics*, a quarterly dedicated to "connecting research with practice, to connecting teachers with research and researchers with the reality of the classroom, and by doing so, making adult basic education research more relevant to the field" (2001, p. 2).

Examples of State Professional Development Systems

In Pennsylvania, the Bureau of Adult Basic and Literacy Education (ABLE) provides state leadership activities to adult educators through six regional professional development centers across the state. They provide regional and statewide learning opportunities in workshops and through on-line delivery, and they work with the Pennsylvania Association for Adult Continuing Education (PAACE), a professional association, to maintain a learning network for professionals.

In Washington State, EFF has been the umbrella under which adult educators, program managers, community-based program staff, and parents have received professional development through a project called Families That Work, which is organized by the state's department of human services. Intensive EFF training has brought together partners in this family literacy initiative, providing opportunities for individual peer exchange and mentoring in addition to quarterly retreats that address both the instructional and administrative components of programs so that "everyone is speaking the same language and seeking the same results: effective parents who are able to provide for their families" (National Institute for Literacy, 2002, p. 12).

In the Northwest, states share professional development resources and services through the regional collaboration of the Northwest Regional Literacy Resource Center (NWRLRC), which was established in 1993. This partnership offers multistate strategies for technical assistance to improve the quality of adult education practice in Montana, Idaho, Oregon, Wyoming, Washington, and Alaska.

In New York State, we have established a network of staff development professionals who operate regionally, advised by local advisory boards under the direction of the state's education department. Local "consortia" of adult education professionals provide constant input on their current and future needs and wants in order to improve practice and program operation. This input is mixed with directives from state education initiatives, which are derived from national trends and directions. The result is a unified system of delivery that reflects local needs, individual needs, and statewide direction that is consistent with national trends. Practitioners are surveyed and also provide input through conversation and focus groups. This aggregate information influences programming content and delivery format. Regional strategic plans are established and revised through ongoing needs analysis and activity evaluations. This structured yet flexible system permits consistent and up-to-date delivery of professional services to adult educators in the state.

Across the country and in New York State, the delivery formats vary from workshop-type sessions to regional and distance-learning conferences to individual practitioner research and peer-sharing activities. Often, national initiatives—such as on learning disabilities, standards, the National

Reporting System, and the GED test—influence the professional development topics covered. Effective staff developers translate such topics into programming that those local and regional programs can assimilate and translate into practice readily. The commonly desired end is to improve practice and increase learners' skill mastery and life-transforming knowledge acquisition. This purpose is part of what makes the field of adult education such a transparent yet influential force in society. Professional development can influence the learners educators work with through personal satisfaction, job promotion, improved parenting skills, and greater civic participation (Robertson, 1996; Sparks and Hirsh, 1997).

Recommendations for Professional Development

Adult educators who participate in staff development activities often ask for hands-on techniques that they can "take back and implement immediately" with their students. In our staff development work we have seen that, because only limited time is allotted by agencies for staff development and because it is often unpaid time, educators want current research that has been translated into immediately applicable, practical tools for their work. The part-time instructor, volunteer tutor, or full-time staff person with contact hours and student progress reports to maintain has a very specific purpose for participating in professional development—to obtain information, techniques, and resources that are research-based, classroom-proven, low-cost, and accessible. A professional developer's task is to locate, evaluate, disseminate, and instruct in the purpose and use of such resources, which derive from research performed by university- or practitioner-based efforts. This focused purpose distinguishes professional development from the academic study of adult education, which seeks to extend the field's knowledge and theory base in addition to serving the needs of practitioners. This volume, too, will help us focus on the teachers of adults' needs as adult learners themselves.

Field-Based Research. The professional development phenomenon of relying on materials and resources from peers has been gaining prominence in the field of adult education. One example is the Pennsylvania Adult Literacy Practitioner Inquiry Network (PALPIN). Other states, such as Kentucky and California, have ongoing practitioner research projects that they then share with the field in statewide conferences. New York State uses the peer review process, where educators develop and share with peers "learning experiences" that are standards-based activities for adult educators. Colleagues review the learning experiences that are then revised and enhanced by the author. The learning experiences are then shared with the field. In addition, the Literacy Assistance Center in New York City awards minigrants on a regular basis to educators for inquiry research. Researchers present their work and findings in forums, on-line, and in print formats. Titles of recent studies were "Assessing the Viability of the Spanish GED in

New York City" and "Narrowing the Digital Divide Between Adult ESOL Learners and Their Children" (Kaplan, 2001). Having participated in the New England Literacy Assistance Center's Web site and technology projects, we have shared and further developed these efforts in our region with local educators. The process of first learning alongside regional practitioners from the New York and New England areas, and then continuing the research and implementation with local educators, is exciting and connects one's perspectives to the national level.

The impetus for conducting local practitioner research comes from a need to solve program-based problems and develop a plan for improvement supported by data gathered, at times, with student participation. According to anecdotal reports from participants in research projects in Pennsylvania, they have "a more questioning attitude and are more willing to examine their practice" and see their action research as program improvement and "as meaningful, not futile, attempts" (Weirauch and Kuhne, 2001, p. 10). The personal professional impact is evident, and the challenge for the field is to develop venues for wider sharing of research results and stimulating further inquiry research projects by educators (Kuhne and Quigley, 1997).

Reflective Practice. Developing a personal philosophy of adult education complements encouraging practitioner research and program-based problem solving. The adult education staff developer grounds practitioners in philosophy based on early researchers such as Lindeman (1926) and more recent work by Mezirow (1998) and Brookfield (1995), allowing educators the opportunity to reflect and develop personal perspectives on the roles of educators and students and the purpose of education. As educators begin to reflect on what they say they believe, and compare it with how they *actually* engage in instruction with students, they develop a new awareness of what creates an effective learning and teaching environment.

Developing a philosophy and being exposed to accomplished researchers in the field give new practitioners a sense of professionalism. This engages their original interest in teaching adults, can inspire additional university-level pursuits, and can lead to career opportunities in program administration. Thus, discussion of philosophy and research and their relationship to instructional practice should be included in new practitioner in-services and in later seminars on instructional delivery, student motivation, and assessment.

Learner-Driven Instruction. Central to adult education philosophy is the concept of learner-centered, participatory learning, with the teacher taking on the role of facilitator (Brookfield, 1986; Mezirow, 1998). Learners take part in decision making about learning goals and the teacher supports this collective learning. In this critical or humanist philosophy, the teacher connects the learner's experiences to the topic through critical reflection and discourse. The educator fosters discussion to allow learners to think for themselves, to evaluate assumptions or "where people are coming from," in order to validate beliefs, intentions, and values. The learners make changes in their lives based on gaining new knowledge and learning to become more engaged, aware citizens in a democratic society. Adult educators can once again connect with their original desire to help adults participate more fully in society and live fuller lives through learner-centered instruction.

Technology provides a contextual example of how a staff developer can model learner-centered practices. Learners—in this case, teachers of adults—might indicate through surveys their desire to learn to use technology in their workplace. A staff developer creates programming that models sound, innovative technological applications for their teaching. The loop of feedback of learner needs, tailored instruction, and applied new knowledge—similar to the methodologies we encourage using with adult students—is completed. For example, I am currently working with a math practitioner who has presented very successfully in our past regional and state workshops. We would like to embrace videoconferencing as a new format that would make needed learning accessible to greater numbers of teachers, and we will soon be delivering GED math-related sessions in this way. However, my friend and math expert needs ample support to reach a comfort level with the medium, and I, as the staff developer, must facilitate this for him. I hope he will then feel confident enough to venture into this and other technological media to enhance his practice with his students as well.

Conclusion

Practitioner-driven staff development that models effective adult education practice offers participants a sense of involvement and ownership in a profession that often presents more challenges than opportunities. A parallel comparison can be made with adult learners and adult educators in that they are underserved in their respective educational systems. This can be overcome by creating a staff development system where practitioners are an integral part of the process for student achievement improvement. A 2001 National Institute for Literacy survey describes states' needs in the area of improving the quality and delivery of professional development for adult educators. Along with more funding and time off for staff training, states are seeking models, evaluation strategies, and information about other successful state professional development systems and how to replicate them or improve on them.

According to the NIFL survey, professional development programs are needed that cover the accountability requirements of the National Reporting System, instructional topics of GED 2002, the Equipped for the Future program, teaching people with learning disabilities, incorporating technology, and meeting the demands of a growing ESOL adult learner population. In New York our regional and statewide practitioner surveys also indicate an urgent need for professional development in the area of including younger learners, those ages sixteen to twenty-one, in the adult education system, as increased numbers of them drop out of high school because of stricter K–12 standards and graduating requirements.

Unified, well-funded systems that build on the expertise of educators and methodologies grounded in adult learning theory can support and validate the tremendous efforts of the professionals working in adult basic education in the United States. Increased learner achievement and practitioner leadership in the field are the goals and the rewards of good professional development practice.

References

Brookfield, S. *Understanding and Facilitating Adult Learning.* San Francisco: Jossey-Bass, 1986.

Brookfield, S. *Becoming a Critically Reflective Thinker.* San Francisco: Jossey-Bass, 1995.

Kaplan, A. "NYCPDC Update." *Literacy Update,* 2001, *11*(1), 3.

Kuhne, G., and Quigley, A. "A Condition That Is Not Yet: Reactions, Reflections, and Closing Comments." In G. Kuhne and A. Quigley (eds.), *Creating Practical Knowledge Through Action Research: Posing Problems, Solving Problems, and Improving Daily Practice.* San Francisco: Jossey-Bass, 1997.

Kutner, M., and Tibbetts, J. *Looking to the Future: Components of a Comprehensive Professional Development System for Adult Educators.* Washington, D.C.: Pelavin Research Institute, 1997.

Lindeman, E. C. *The Meaning of Adult Education.* New York: New Republic, 1926.

Mezirow, J. "On Critical Reflection." *Adult Education Quarterly,* 1998, *48*(3), 185–198.

National Center for the Study of Adult Learning and Literacy. "Masthead." *Focus on Basics,* 2001, *4*(D), 5. [http://www.gse.harvard.edu/~ncsall/fob/2001/mast_apr.html].

National Institute for Literacy. "EFF Links Washington's Families That Work Initiative." *EFF Voice,* Winter 2002, *3*(1), 12.

National Institute for Literacy. *NIFL Policy Updates.* Mar. 2002. [http://www.nifl.gov/lincs/collections/policy.html].

Robertson, D. "Facilitating Transformative Learning: Attending to the Dynamics of the Educational Helping Relationship." *Adult Education Quarterly,* 1996, *47*(1), 42–45.

Smith, C., Hofer, J., and Gillespie, M. "The Working Conditions of Adult Literacy Teachers: Preliminary Findings from the NCSALL Staff Development Study." *Focus on Basics,* 2001, *4*(D). [http://www.gse.harvard.edu/~ncsall/fob/2001/smith.html].

Sparks, D., and Hirsh, S. *A New Vision for Staff Development.* Alexandria, Va.: Association for Supervision and Curriculum Development, 1997.

Tolbert, M. *Professional Development for Adult Education Instructors: State Policy Update.* Washington, D.C.: National Institute for Literacy, Dec. 2001.

Weirauch, M., and Kuhne, G. "Satisfying the Itch: Addressing Problems in Adult Literacy Programs with Action Research." *Adult Learning,* 2001, *11*(3), 9–11.

GEORGES MARCEAU is executive director of the Central New York Staff Development Consortium in Syracuse, New York, and immediate past president of the New York Association of Community Continuing Education.

9

This chapter looks at the new demands on trainers in corporate settings and provides examples that illustrate the skills and abilities that should become part of their professional development. It concludes with recommendations based on principles of adult learning and organization development.

Professional Development in Corporate Training

Susan R. Meyer, Victoria J. Marsick

Globalization, technology development, and the changing nature of work in corporations have widespread implications for the professional development of trainers, their capabilities, and their connection with organizations. In the past decade, shifts in management style, greater diversity among learners, and an increased emphasis on learning and knowledge management in organizations have broadened and changed the role and positioning of training. In this chapter we provide examples to illustrate the new demands on trainers and draw from these examples the skills and abilities that should be included in the professional development of trainers today. We conclude with recommendations about how to develop trainers using principles of adult learning and organization development.

Description of Practice and Field

The challenges that trainers and other educators of adults face in corporate settings are greater than ever because of the variety and range of the learning experiences their clients need. Furthermore, educators of adults must increasingly align training with the organizational mission and goals, and they must meet demands for accountability and fiscal responsibility. Learning is more often integrated with work through training designs that incorporate coaching, mentoring, and self-directed learning. People are learning through desktop technologies, using distance or e-learning, and

Permission was received from all persons identified in this chapter to use their names and those of their organizations.

participating in shorter, more focused training activities. In consequence, trainers need more varied skills, greater flexibility, and the ability to diagnose and adapt to situations rapidly.

We see a demand emerging in today's workplace for blending adult learning principles with organization development principles. Trainers must be conversant with both. A shift toward creating learning activities rather than stand-alone training programs also requires greater flexibility on the part of trainers and the ability to translate information from subject matter experts in order to meet very local, contextualized needs for learning that are integrated with work. The literature that seems most relevant is that on self-directed learning, because individuals are increasingly becoming free-agent learners (Cauldron, 1999). At the same time, there is also a recognition that people learn best in organizations because they are members of overlapping communities of practice (Wenger, 1998).

The Changing Nature of Training

The following four examples illustrate how training is changing and show how the professional development needs of trainers are changing too. Although each story comes from a different setting, they all show that training is now embedded in ongoing work. The first example emphasizes the trainer's need to modularize learning so that it is truly learner-centered. The second focuses on the need to model the skills of reflective practice and joint learning. The third shows how experiential learning can help people learn effectively in context. The fourth focuses on the link between adult learning and organizational change.

Professionalizing Product Training. A software company had no formal product training for its clients. Because part of the job of its new learning and development department was to educate clients on how to use the software they were purchasing, the lack of product training was a real problem that had to be solved in an extremely tight time frame. For the newly hired director of the department, this was the first priority. This woman's background was not in software development or marketing, but as she maintained, a good trainer "doesn't need to know what you know, but can help you do your work better."

The director's challenge was to move from no curriculum to core classroom-based programs that would enable people to sell products, and to do it in three months. She needed a design that would be meaningful to technical people and could be delivered in short programs. One problem was that knowledge was tightly held in this organization. The organization's strengths were technical, not interpersonal. There was low turnover, and the idea of pooling information was simply foreign. Leadership was not perceived to invite participation in decision making.

The director hired people with strong technical skills (to balance her own strong training development skills) and some basic understanding of training. She needed staff who could understand her design framework but who could also communicate in the language of the technical experts and use high-end software. In researching design options, she discovered Reusable Learning Objects (RLOs), a concept introduced to her by Cisco Systems. It describes core concepts that can be clustered to create variable-length (modularized) training on demand.

The director and her staff needed to collect information to develop training programs while simultaneously making sense of the relationships between the pieces. She brought together eight key people for two days in an intensive think-tank session kicked off by the CEO. A series of focused questions allowed the group to get to know each other and find out what others knew as well as identify customer knowledge and needs. Participants worked with partners, using different scenarios, to decide on RLOs in predetermined categories. The thirty-six RLOs scoped out in this process were grouped and developed into three courses. Individuals across department lines learned to work together in an entirely new way. They broke through organizational silos and learned the advantages of freely sharing information.

Mentoring and Management Development. Acknowledging that some managerial skills cannot be taught in the classroom, New York City's Department of Personnel supplemented its managerial and supervisory certificate programs with a mentoring program. Because some mentors did not have the required skills, trainers therefore needed the skills to teach both mentors and mentees how to create and maintain a learning dialogue.

In order to make successful matches, trainers had to use interview and written data to identify mentor and mentee candidates and then match learning needs with teaching strengths across agency and job function. The challenge in maintaining the program was for training staff to learn how to facilitate the relationships over an eighteen-month period. This meant that they had to learn how to enter into reflective dialogue and also become relationship managers.

A second mentoring program was set up in the Metropolitan Transportation Authority's Department of Buses. The program was designed to help managers move up quickly in the organization and move effortlessly between three distinct subcultures in the organization. Unfortunately, knowledge was rarely shared across these subcultures, or at the middle- to senior-management levels. These knowledge gaps had a significant impact on performance.

Pat O'Brien, then vice president of buses, asked for help in addressing this problem. She was sure that mentoring was the appropriate solution and wanted help in designing and implementing a structured mentoring program. Because she wanted to underscore the reciprocal nature of shared learning in the program, she created an advisory group with volunteers from different units and with different job titles.

Organizations often require measurements of learning. The Department of Buses' program included clear goals and objectives and milestone reports, combined with a structured reflective practicum. Participants were chosen from different areas and worked together on a project that would both benefit the department and increase the mentees' knowledge of the mentors' area. The projects resulted in measurable evidence of learning and concomitant cost benefits to the organizations. Examples include a stress-reduction video with stretching exercises that drivers can do on their buses and a process for presenting statistical data to line staff in a way that is meaningful to them and that has resulted in improved on-time performance.

Creating a New Corporate Venture. In 1992 Sony introduced "Sony Style," a marketing concept and a retail store, to the New York City marketplace. It was a joint venture between three Sony entities: music, pictures, and hardware. Wanda Morrison, learning and development manager, faced a variety of new situations, including creating a new group and culture from a blend of three cultures; gaining buy-in and collaboration from all parties associated with the project; understanding what it means to become a retailer rather than a manufacturer of products and services; and gaining commitment, support, and visibility of management. This required thinking differently about learning. Morrison's group needed to recognize that learning comes from many places and that facilitating learning would require adapting quickly and adjusting to different ways of thinking across constituencies. In effect, they became responsible for translating among multiple points of view on a situation in order to build a common knowledge base.

The learning methods and techniques Morrison employed were varied but all emphasized experiential principles. Sales associates had to keep abreast of their technical product categories and become cross-trained in related categories. Also, because of their central location in New York City, they had to become adept at giving directions to popular tourist locations. Sales associates were "trained" by taking "a walk in the city" with cameras to document destination points of their choice. They were helped to link sales objectives and rapport-building techniques to create a more comfortable consumer and sales associate relationship. They never lost the focus on rapport building, even when the outcome was not a sale.

A cross-cultural experiential exercise helped sales associates understand how cultures use different gestures, have different body language and customs, and take offense and are slighted by different things. This information was translated into techniques for working successfully with a multicultural clientele.

Because a broad knowledge base was crucial to the success of the store, sales associates were paired across areas of expertise to work together in study groups. Compensation was structured for collaboration instead of competition. Senior management from Sony collaborated to test the knowledge level of the sales associates informally. Collaboration was modeled at all levels.

Morrison reported a variety of lessons learned by herself and her staff: sales associates needed to acknowledge multiple organizational cultures, have good listening skills, and be willing to adapt and change as a project began to take on a life of its own. Management needed to provide opportunities for the group to add to the life of the project, allow members to bring their own creativity to the process, and finally, not lose sight of the goal.

Action Learning. For three years, New York City's Transit Authority has used action learning to help senior managers focus on concrete problems in an environment of open communication, team learning, and critical reflection. The literature (Marquardt, 1999, 1997; Watkins and Marsick, 1996; Yorks, O'Neil, and Marsick, 1999) shows the effectiveness of action learning in providing a forum for solving difficult organizational problems. The Transit Authority continues to grapple with the need to become increasingly flexible and responsive in a climate of change. This highly structured, hierarchical, paramilitary-like organization, which sought to improve succession planning and broaden the pool of managers involved in innovating, problem solving, and decision making, decided to take an innovative approach. The senior vice president for subways wanted a program that would begin to break down organizational norms against open cross-divisional communication, promote systems thinking, and change managerial practices.

In scope, design, and duration, the general superintendents' program represented a complete departure from how training had previously been conducted for any group in the organization. It was the first time that managers had been asked to deal with large-scale organizational problems. It was the first time that they had been brought together for as long as two weeks. Many felt it was the first time that anyone had really cared about what they thought. The design was ambitious in that the program sought to effect real change in the organization.

The program presented several challenges for the training group. This was a very different kind of program. It required cycles of training, research, discussion, and reflection, which meant having training staff available for long periods of time without having them actually do any training. It required strong facilitation skills rather than strong delivery skills. The trainers would have to remove themselves from the decision-making task while being highly attentive to process issues.

Yorks, O'Neil, and Marsick (1999) note that some models of action learning place a stronger emphasis on the role of intentional, explicit reflection than others. The intent of the design of this program was to encourage participants to form initial hypotheses about the causes of problems set out by the senior vice president.

Five groups of fifteen general superintendents met in six facilitated action learning settings and as a large group over a ten-day period.

Participants were selected from each of the divisions of the Department of Subways. Groups were formed to reflect the widest possible diversity in job function, gender, ethnicity, and age. Each group was assigned a concern. In a series of cycles, they investigated the problems, reported findings, reflected on what they had learned and how that affected their understanding of the problem and the organization, and then continued to research. Finally, each group generated a proposal outlining solutions that was reviewed by executive management. The groups were then charged with implementing the solutions over the course of a year.

Impact

The initiatives described here suggest that trainers need to acquire and model the capabilities that they are teaching in organizations. We recommend that the professional development of trainers be carried out using similar principles and similar practices of adult learning and organizational development. This means that university-based, certificate, and in-service programs need to be designed as learning laboratories.

All of the case examples illustrate that trainers need to experience the changing organizational conditions they will be working in. As they do, we believe that they will need help in three areas: using reflective practice skills to make sense of their situation, as illustrated in the Sony example; tailoring learning solutions to their own and other local learning needs, as illustrated in the Department of Buses and the software company examples; and developing and nurturing collaborative communities of practice, as illustrated in the Department of Subways example.

Trainers need capabilities that are both broader and deeper than when learning initiatives were confined to workshops and highly structured activities. Increasingly, organizations are relying less on formal classroom-based training sessions alone and are adopting innovative learning programs. Yet there will always be a need for well-crafted classroom-based programs.

Trainers now need much more than delivery and design skills. They must be strategic partners with line and senior management. They need a deep understanding of diverse clients and their different learning styles. They must be able to read the context, assess needs, and select or create appropriate mini–learning sessions that are often delivered just in time in the middle of work cycles. They also need to understand how development of individuals promotes and contributes to group and organizational learning.

Often trainers are asked to forge links among constituencies inside and outside the organization. They need help translating from one organizational language to another, as in the mentoring examples, or from technology to plain English, as in the software company example.

Trainers are becoming involved with their clients in different ways. They are serving as advisers on a long-term basis. The action learning example shows us that trainers are supporting work projects rather than simply transmitting the skills necessary to do the project work.

The need to relate to clients in multiple contexts and over longer periods of time creates a need to rethink the trainer's job description and to look at costing out training initiatives differently. Although teaching employees how to be more productive remains central to training, the emphasis has broadened from concrete job skills to interpersonal and learning skills. Programs address how employees work together and how they think together.

Recommendations

What does all this mean for training and development professionals and their preparation? It means that both a solid foundation in traditional training design and delivery and a vast array of innovative techniques must be included in trainer preparation. It means that the abilities to think both quickly and creatively, to envision alternative ways to shape the same material, and to assess, analyze, and rethink in the moment are becoming core competencies.

The professional development of trainers should still include the basics of design and delivery—needs assessment, developing objectives, creating an agenda, selecting appropriate activities, providing for transfer, and designing and conducting evaluation activities. The approach to teaching these basics, however, has evolved over time to move beyond instrumental learning. Trainers are increasingly being encouraged to look at programs from multiple perspectives. As we saw in the Sony example, they are beginning to consider diversity, learning how to learn, and sharing information across departments.

According to Riddle (2000), training is critical in five areas today. These areas—stimulating creativity, assessing innovation options, focusing on the customer, designing new services, and implementing change—require a broad range of skills on the part of the trainer. Development of trainers should include demonstrating multiple approaches to delivering the same information. Trainers need to learn how to move past using needs assessment to identify deficits to analyzing employee experiences and translating them into meaningful training activities. Activities increasingly involve active experiential learning and debriefings.

Development must also prepare trainers to use more than one delivery system. In the future, they will have to be as comfortable in front of a camera or on-line as they are in the classroom. This means they will have to become better at identifying core learning and creating multiple representations of the same information.

Training is moving out of the classroom in other directions as well. We see learning spaces being created on shop floors and in simulators. As the control of learning returns to the learner in more situations, the developers of trainers will need to revisit self-directed learning to create better ways to inject opportunities for reflection, clarification, and guidance.

Finally, trainer development should address the trainer's ability to help learners integrate information gathered in a variety of settings into a coherent body. How will classroom learning, independent reading, and experimentation at the computer or on the shop floor be pulled together into a meaningful whole? We must prepare trainers to become increasingly capable of synthesizing multiple points of view and of passing those skills on to create thinking, learning, productive employees.

References

Cauldron, S. "Free Agent Learner." *Training and Development,* 1999, 52(8), 26–31.

Marquardt, M. *Action Learning.* Alexandria, Va.: American Society for Training and Development, 1997.

Marquardt, M. *Action Learning in Action: Transforming Problems and People for World-Class Organizational Learning.* Palo Alto, Calif.: Davies-Black, 1999.

Riddle, D. "Innovate: How Services Exporters Survive and Thrive in the New Millennium." *International Trade Forum,* 2000, 4, 17.

Watkins, K. E., and Marsick, V. J. *In Action: Creating the Learning Organization.* Alexandria, Va.: American Society for Training and Development, 1996.

Wenger, E. *Communities of Practice: Learning, Meaning, and Identity.* Cambridge: Cambridge University Press, 1998.

Yorks, L., O'Neil, J., and Marsick, V. J. *Action Learning: Successful Strategies for Individual, Team, and Organizational Development.* Baton Rouge, La.: Academy of Human Resource Development, 1999.

SUSAN R. MEYER *is principal in the BoschMeyer Consulting Group and adjunct assistant professor of adult education and organizational learning, Department of Organization and Leadership, Teachers College, Columbia University, New York City.*

VICTORIA J. MARSICK *is codirector (with Martha A. Gephart) of the J. M. Huber Institute for Learning in Organizations and professor of adult education and organizational learning, Department of Organization and Leadership, Teachers College, Columbia University, New York City.*

10

Bringing together the themes and perspectives presented in this sourcebook, the authors offer a new vision for professional development and recommendations to help prepare those who work with teachers of adults to meet the challenges and changes.

Changes, Challenges, and the Future

Patricia A. Lawler, Kathleen P. King

Teachers of adults practice in diverse settings. In this volume we have seen their work and their challenges in higher education, adult basic education, and the workplace. In many cases these faculty, teachers, and trainers have had little or no training in working with adult learners. They themselves come from diverse backgrounds, educational experiences, and cultural contexts. Their charge is to promote learning and change in the adults they teach. They work in complex organizations, ranging from universities to large corporations to community volunteer groups. They may find support for their endeavors in their organizations or they may find that they are on their own as they set out to teach and train their adult students.

We saw in earlier chapters a trend toward the professional development of teachers of adults, a trend that no longer looks like what we have done all along. Colleges and universities are not just expanding their professional development offerings to their faculty but also shifting the focus—from teaching to learning, and from traditional delivery systems to technology-enhanced pedagogy. Adult basic education providers are networking and collaborating to meet the needs of the teachers, trainers, and volunteers who serve adults who have limited educational experiences. In the corporate world, trainers are being challenged by new and innovative ways to deliver training and enhance skills in the workplace.

In all of these instances it is clear that teachers of adults have challenging work ahead of them and that little or no attention is being paid to their own learning needs and conditions. With this in mind, we now address this deficit, seek to support this group who may not been thought of as adult learners in the past, and provide a new vision for their professional development.

NEW DIRECTIONS FOR ADULT AND CONTINUING EDUCATION, no. 98, Summer 2003 © Wiley Periodicals, Inc.

Changes and Challenges: A Review

The authors of this volume have enumerated the changes and challenges facing those who work in professional development with teachers of adults. To ensure that teachers of adults succeed with their diverse populations in this changing context, we proposed a new perspective for their professional development based on sound adult learning principles. In this conceptual framework, we see teachers of adults as adult learners themselves. Using the principles and strategies of adult learning in a professional development context provides practitioners with new ways to integrate theory and practice and approach old problems. In reviewing our authors' proposals, we build a new vision for professional development and make several recommendations for the future.

In her discussion on theory and practice in Chapter Three, Daley demonstrates how learner-centered teaching and learning could find an effective place in professional development. Taking what we know succeeds in the traditional adult education classroom, she expands the concept to inform professional development. Our theories of teaching and learning for adults need to be consistent with our current professional development planning and delivery practices for teachers of adults.

Transformative learning has been the subject of intense discussion in adult education circles for the last twenty years. In Chapter Four, Cranton and King expand this discussion into the professional development arena. If we view teachers of adults as adult learners and incorporate transformative learning strategies, then personal learning and development moves front and center, and the role of reflective practice becomes paramount. Professional development that includes critical self-reflection on performance, values, beliefs, and assumptions provides a different vantage point for practice than most of the models of practice we are familiar with in this field. Adult learning principles, learner-centered teaching and learning, and transformative learning thus support the conceptual development of professional development as adult learning.

This sourcebook goes even further in extending the theoretical discussion to today's practical challenges. Certainly, motivating teachers of adults in their professional development and helping them to incorporate technology with their own learners are two of our most pressing challenges. In Chapter Five Wlodkowski gives us some help with his Motivational Framework for Culturally Responsive Teaching. He suggests that this model will work with diverse populations in all adult education classrooms and that using it will lead to a learning environment that all adults can accept. Participating teachers of adults are more likely to be motivated if his guidelines are followed: establishing inclusion, developing attitude, enhancing meaning, and engendering competence. For teachers of adults to be motivated to change and to use new learning, Wlodkowski outlines approaches to increase transfer of learning.

In Chapter Six King goes further, linking adult learning theory and professional development practice by providing the journey of transformation as a model of how teachers of adults might engage in learning educational technology and experiencing transformative learning at the same time. This model builds on our understanding of the emotional, rational, and specific concerns that educators may experience while learning and provides a picture of the educator as an adult learner with some familiar concerns: risk, loss, embarrassment, and fear. As we learn to use new technologies in the classroom, we can also learn much about ourselves as learners and teachers. Professional development in technology can mean more than skill attainment, and King's specific recommendations can result in our transforming ourselves during this journey.

Until now we have been speaking of teachers of adults in a general context. However, it is in the specific contexts that an adult learning approach to their professional development especially comes alive for us. The next chapters in the book discuss professional development in the distinct settings of higher education, adult basic education, and corporate training. As the authors considered the current needs and theoretical roots of their individual contexts, they explained how teaching adults involves specific issues for both the teachers and their professional developers. From this perspective each author was then able to formulate recommendations that were pertinent to those particular conditions. In higher education, Brancato (Chapter Seven) presents the learning organization (Senge, 1990) as a significant influence on how institutions may reconcile and promote professional development for teachers of adults as adult learning. The main tenets of personal mastery, team learning, mental models, shared vision, and systems thinking frame her recommendations for practice. Learning organizations that focus on the learning needs of their employees can find a consistent and powerful validation of their purposes. She sees this as being compatible with higher education today and goes so far as to say that this is the way to work with faculty in a broader, more comprehensive context.

The adult basic education context is the next distinct setting for professional development of teachers of adults, discussed by Marceau in Chapter Eight. Dominated by test scores and performance assessment, these literacy, ESOL, and GED programs center first and foremost on outcomes. Here we run the risk of losing sight of the big teaching-and-learning picture, as well as of the needs of educators themselves. Marceau demonstrates how the needs of these teachers of adults can be addressed through targeted professional development initiatives grounded in adult learning principles. His basic but far-reaching recommendations include field-based research, reflective practice, and learner-driven instruction. He helps us recognize that classroom and learner (teacher) needs must remain a primary focus in planning professional development for these educators.

Finally, we look at workplace education and human resource development in Chapter Nine. Meyer and Marsick present an adult learning perspective in four different workplace organizations that are engaged in planning and delivering training. Their cases illustrate the changing nature of training in corporate settings. They provide four illustrations: product training, mentoring and management development, new corporate ventures, and action learning. These cases demonstrate how adult learning and organization development principles are key to the successful professional development of these teachers of adults.

A New Vision for Professional Development of Teachers of Adults

This volume's discussion leads to a new vision for professional development of teachers of adults. As we work with more and more faculty, trainers, and teachers we have found that they respond enthusiastically to the Adult Learning Model for Faculty Development presented earlier in this volume. However, with the varied contexts, there is more to consider.

There is a need for a new vision in professional development. The issues, trends, challenges, and changing contexts described in this volume make it quite clear to those of us working in the field that new ideas and new strategies are needed. Although the institutions and organizations where adult education takes place are also responding to change, we as professional developers have the opportunity to be proactive leaders (Eckel, 2002). We can do this by paying attention to our own personal development, by setting a new and important agenda for learning, and by modeling sound educational practices. "Continual challenges of change within a community that has undergone and is still undergoing speedy and significant change, can and do impinge on the personal development of the individual, and this impingement reflects on the performance of the institution" (Nicholls, 2001, p. 13). If as professional developers we respond to this call for proactive leadership, we will have to take risks and challenge the status quo as we deliver this new vision for professional development. Challenging the status quo can begin with a new commitment to professional development from three perspectives.

The first perspective is to reconceptualize the professional development process to include an understanding of teachers of adults and the context in which they work. For some time now, our focus has been on content: what the teacher of adults should learn, a new platform for online courses, recent scholarship in a discipline, or a new schema for teaching reading. Our focus has also been on assessment, accountability, and outcomes. Now we need to enlarge our focus. We need to start with our teachers of adults, understanding their needs, motivations, goals, and reward structures. We must also consider their organizational context. Planning programs in professional development, like other adult education programming, is a social activity; the context of people, politics, and organizational culture plays an integral role (Cevero and Wilson, 1994). Unless we pay attention to the context, we lose sight of the whole picture and may miss what is really important for our teachers and trainers to be successful in their new learning and changing behaviors (Lawler and King, 2000). We can do this by scanning the environment, conducting formal and informal needs assessment, and becoming familiar with all aspects of our teachers' work roles and the changing demands in their professional lives. This new perspective demands that we become reflective in our practice, questioning not only our assumptions about teachers of adults and professional development but also our assumptions about the organization, the cultural context, and professional development itself.

Renewing our commitment requires a second perspective: integrating the concept of active learning into our professional development activities. Research has shown that adults who are active in their learning "will be more likely to incorporate what they are learning in personally meaningful ways" (Myers and Jones, 1993, p. 32). When our teachers of adults actively participate in professional development activities, we take a more collaborative approach. Our participants may be engaged both in developing programs and in the training seminar or workshop classroom. This will require a change in how we view ourselves and our role as professional developers (Myers and Jones, 1993). Here again we are challenged to take risks. We need to consider how our teachers learn, their diverse learning styles, and the motivation that will enhance transfer of learning. We begin to create strategies for engagement in the learning activities and invite our teachers of adults into the planning and evaluation process. Rather than managers and experts, we become listeners, questioners, and reflective collaborators. This means that we move away from always being in charge and become more team-oriented, as Senge (1990) urges those in a learning organization to be.

The third perspective—reflection and dialogue—requires that we understand ourselves as professional developers, that we become aware of our own practice and our skills of questioning and listening. Adult education writers (Brookfield, 1995; Mezirow and Associates, 1990) explain that when we reflect on our actions and the world around us it encourages learning. As professional developers we have the opportunity to develop our practice. Nicholls (2001) proposes that if this development is "a process including personal and professional growth, then critical reflection on practice will be central to learning" (p. 61). We are back to risk taking as we come to understand our role and influence in the cultural context of professional development. We observe, reflect, and take action at each step of the process in working with our teachers of adults. Asking questions about the effects of what we are doing, and seeking both positive and negative answers are tasks for professional developers who are creating a new vision. As we pick our way through the labyrinth of programs for teachers of adults, we do more than deliver content and skill acquisition opportunities. We have an opportunity to model as reflective practitioners (Schön, 1983)

Figure 10.1. Integrative Approach to Professional Development

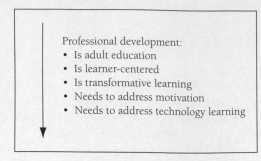

Professional development:
• Is adult education
• Is learner-centered
• Is transformative learning
• Needs to address motivation
• Needs to address technology learning

working with adult learners to enhance the professional development experience.

Our new vision for professional development with teachers of adults leads us in a direction to enhance our practice. This vision is based on and proceeds from five assumptions; this relationship is illustrated in Figure 10.1.

First, professional development is adult education. Although this may seem obvious now, it has been our experience that those working in professional development with teachers of adults, those observing programs, and those responsible for the organizations in which professional development takes place do not see it as adult education. When suggested that this work really is adult education, many are surprised that they never thought of it that way. Most concentrate on the adult learners that these teachers work with in their practice, not on the teachers themselves. We can and should certainly tap into the wealth of research, literature, and practical application from the discipline of adult education in the work we do in professional development.

The second assumption requires us to change our teaching and learning paradigm. We now are moving to a learner-centered philosophy and practice of adult education. Teachers of adults—our learners—are now at the center of the educational transaction. Their characteristics, needs, goals, issues, and context are now front and center in the planning, development, and delivery of our professional development programs. We move to a more facilitative role in a collaborative programming process.

We now come to the third assumption, that professional development is transformative learning. As we view teachers of adults as adult learners we can also view professional development as transformative learning. Looking at professional development as an opportunity to cultivate reflective practice, challenge assumptions, beliefs, and values, and engage in meaning-making brings an entirely different dimension to what is at stake. Professional development can be a lifelong process and a way to empower individuals to transform themselves and their perspectives.

The fourth and fifth assumptions arise from two ubiquitous challenges that face professional development. Based on experience and the literature, participant motivation and technology learning continually appear as critical needs in the professional development of educators of adults. Motivation has always been key to learning and change. We need to understand the unique issues for teachers of adults. Again, relying on the fields of adult learning and motivation, we can tap into the theories and practical strategies used with adult learners. Taking these concepts and applying them to professional development assists our understanding of why teachers, trainers, faculty, and volunteers are reluctant to change and grow in their practice with their adult students.

Finally, we assume that the need for learning educational technology pressures educators continually. Rapidly changing technology has been greatly affecting our personal and professional lives for many years. Those involved in the education of adults cannot forget the needs, demands, and challenges they and their learners face daily when working with technology. Professional development vision and practice that will endure into the future must possess effective strategies by which to address these challenges. In the trenches, we need to cope with constantly changing technology as users, learners, and educators. Our vision of professional development has to include ways to address these challenges.

Future Issues for Professional Development with Teachers of Adults

As more professional developers come to understand that the work they do really is adult education and that their participants are adult learners, several other issues will need to be addressed. In wrapping up this volume, we suggest that two of these issues point to gaps in our professional practice literature. Filling those gaps will be critical to our moving successfully into the future. If professional development with teachers of adults is to continue to be a positive intervention resulting in enhanced learning and teaching in the various adult education classrooms—from the university to the shop floor to the literacy classroom—then we need to be serious and proactive about these issues.

First, we must seriously look at evaluating our efforts as professional developers. Although most of us ask our participants for immediate feedback after a professional development session is over, we tend not to look at evaluation as one of our main tasks. It is time to take note of what types of evaluation are taking place in professional development. Who does the evaluations? Do we go beyond assessing participant satisfaction? How do we know if transfer of learning and transformative learning take place? What indicators measure best practices? These are but a few of the questions that need to be answered. As monetary constraints collide with advocacy, as a business mentality predominates over academic integrity, and as external stakeholders demand more accountability from our educational organizations, evaluation will be critical. A shift from a deficit model of professional development, where those in charge want us to "fix" what is wrong, to a proactive, growth model, where we see learning as holistic, will demand courage and risk taking on our part. Thorough and useful formative and summative evaluation can provide us with the concrete evidence to state our cases for professional development as adult learning (Lawler and King, 2000).

Models of professional development are lacking in the professional development of teachers of adults. This second gap becomes evident in speaking with professional developers and scanning the literature. Although there are many models of good practice in program planning, training and development, and adult education, there is little that addresses the best practices of professional developers working with teachers of adults. Although we have proposed a new perspective and model based on the premise that professional development is adult learning, we also see the need to ask practitioners what constitutes best practice (Lawler and King, 2000). We encourage professional developers to reflect on their practice, seek opportunities for action research, and question the steps and strategies that constitute their daily work with teachers of adults.

Finally, we encourage professional developers who work with teachers of adults to begin a conversation about their work as adult education. From this new perspective may come new models for improved practice and stronger support to widen the developers' effectiveness with their adult learners: teachers of adults.

References

Brookfield, S. D. *Becoming a Critically Reflective Teacher*. San Francisco: Jossey-Bass, 1995.

Cevero, R. M., and Wilson, A. L. *Planning Responsibly for Adult Education: A Guide to Negotiating Power and Interests*. San Francisco: Jossey-Bass, 1994.

Eckel, P. D. "Institutional Transformation and Change: Insights for Faculty Developers." In D. Lieberman and C. Wehlburg (eds.), *To Improve the Academy* (Vol. 20). Bolton, Mass.: Anker, 2002.

Lawler, P. A., and King, K. P. *Planning for Effective Faculty Development: Using Adult Learning Strategies*. Malabar, Fla.: Krieger, 2000.

Mezirow, J., and Associates. *Fostering Critical Reflection in Adulthood: A Guide to Transformative and Emancipatory Learning*. San Francisco: Jossey-Bass, 1990.

Myers, C., and Jones, T. B. *Promoting Active Learning: Strategies for the College Classroom*. San Francisco: Jossey-Bass, 1993.

Nicholls, G. *Professional Development in Higher Education: New Dimensions and Directions*. Sterling, Va.: Stylus, 2001.

Schön, D. A. *The Reflective Practitioner: How Professionals Think in Action*. New York: Basic Books, 1983.

Senge, P. *The Fifth Discipline: The Art and Practice of the Learning Organization*. New York: Doubleday, 1990.

PATRICIA A. LAWLER *is professor in the Center for Education, Widener University, Chester, Pennsylvania.*

KATHLEEN P. KING *is an associate professor and program director of adult education and human resource development at Fordham University's Graduate School of Education in New York City.*

INDEX

Back Issue/Subscription Order Form

Copy or detach and send to:
Jossey-Bass, A Wiley Company, 989 Market Street, San Francisco CA 94103-1741

Call or fax toll-free: Phone 888-378-2537 6:30AM – 3PM PST; Fax 888-481-2665

Back Issues: Please send me the following issues at $27 each
(Important: please include ISBN number with your order.)

_____

_____

_____

$ _____   Total for single issues

$ _____   SHIPPING CHARGES: SURFACE   Domestic Canadian

		Domestic	Canadian
	First Item	$5.00	$6.00
	Each Add'l Item	$3.00	$1.50

For next-day and second-day delivery rates, call the number listed above.

Subscriptions: Please _start _renew my subscription to *New Directions for Adult and Continuing Education* for the year 2_____at the following rate:

U.S.	_ Individual $70	_ Institutional $149
Canada	_ Individual $70	_ Institutional $189
All Others	_ Individual $94	_ Institutional $223
Online Subscription		_ Institutional $149

**For more information about online subscriptions visit
www.interscience.wiley.com**

$ _____   Total single issues and subscriptions (Add appropriate sales tax for your state for single issue orders. No sales tax for U.S. subscriptions. Canadian residents, add GST for subscriptions and single issues.)

_ Payment enclosed (U.S. check or money order only)
_ VISA _MC _AmEx _# _____ Exp. Date _____

Signature _____ Day Phone _____
_ Bill Me (U.S. institutional orders only. Purchase order required.)

Purchase order # _____
     Federal Tax ID13559302   **GST 89102 8052**

Name _____

Address _____

_____

Phone _____ E-mail _____

For more information about Jossey-Bass, visit our Web site at www.josseybass.com

PROMOTION CODE ND03

ACE93   **Contemporary Viewpoints on Teaching Adults Effectively**
Jovita Ross-Gordon
The aim of this sourcebook was to bring together several authors who have
contributed through their recent publications to the recent literature on
effective teaching of adults. Rather than promoting a single view of what
constitutes good teaching of adults, the chapters challenge each of us to
reflect on our beliefs regarding teaching and learning along with our
understandings of adults learners, the teaching-learning environment, and
the broader social context within which adult continuing education takes
place.
ISBN 0-7879-6229-5

ACE92   **Sociocultural Perspectives on Learning through Work**
Tara Fenwick
Offers an introduction to current themes among academic researchers who
are interested in sociocultural understandings of work-based learning and
working knowledge—how people learn in and through everyday activities
that they think of as work. Explores how learning is embedded in the social
relationships, cultural dynamics, and politics of work, and recommends
different ways for educators to be part of the process.
ISBN 0-7879-5775-5

ACE91   **Understanding and Negotiating the Political Landscape of Adult Education**
Catherine A. Hansman, Peggy A. Sissel
Provides key insights into the politics and policy issues in adult education
today. Offering effective strategies for reflection and action, chapters explore
issues in examination and negotiation of the political aspects of higher
education, adult educators in K–12-focused colleges of education, literacy
education, social welfare reform, professional organizations, and identity of
the field.
ISBN 0-7879-5775-5

ACE90   **Promoting Journal Writing in Adult Education**
Leona M. English, Marie A. Gillen
Exploring the potential for personal growth and learning through journal
writing for student and mentor alike, this volume aims to establish journal
writing as an integral part of the teaching and learning process. Offers
examples of how journal writing can be, and has been, integrated into
educational areas as diverse as health education, higher education, education
for women, and English as a Second Language.
ISBN 0-7879-5774-7

ACE89   **The New Update on Adult Learning Theory**
Sharan B. Merriam
A companion work to 1993's popular An Update on Adult Learning Theory,
this issue examines the developments, research, and continuing scholarship
in self-directed learning. Exploring context-based learning, informal and
incidental learning, somatic learning, and narrative learning, the authors
analyze recent additions to well-established theories and discuss the
potential impact of today's cutting-edge approaches.
ISBN 0-7879-5773-9

ACE83 **The Welfare-to-Work Challenge for Adult Literacy Educators**
Larry G. Martin, James C. Fisher
Welfare reform and workforce development legislation has had a dramatic impact on the funding, implementation, and evaluation of adult basic education and literacy programs. This issue provides a framework for literacy practitioners to better align their field with the demands of the Work First environment and to meet the pragmatic expectations of an extended list of stakeholders.
ISBN 0-7879-1170-4

ACE82 **Providing Culturally Relevant Adult Education: A Challenge for the Twenty-First Century**
Talmadge C. Guy
This issue offers more inclusive theories that focus on how learners construct meaning in a social and cultural context. Chapters identify ways that adult educators can work more effectively with racially, ethnically, and linguistically marginalized learners, and explore how adult education can be an effective tool for empowering learners to take control of their circumstances.
ISBN 0-7879-1167-4

ACE79 **The Power and Potential of Collaborative Learning Partnerships**
Iris M. Saltiel, Angela Sgroi, Ralph G. Brockett
This volume draws on examples of collaborative partnerships to explore the many ways collaboration can generate learning and knowledge. The contributors identify the factors that make for strong collaborative relationships, and they reveal how these partnerships actually help learners generate knowledge and insights well beyond what each brings to the learning situation.
ISBN 0-7879-9815-X

ACE77 **Using Learning to Meet the Challenges of Older Adulthood**
James C. Fisher, Mary Alice Wolf
Combining theory and research in educational gerontology with the practice of older adult learning and education, this volume explores issues related to older adult education in academic and community settings. It is designed for educators and others concerned with the phenomenon of aging in America and with the continuing development of the field of educational gerontology.
ISBN 0-7879-1164-X

ACE75 **Assessing Adult Learning in Diverse Settings: Current Issues and Approaches**
Amy D. Rose, Meredyth A. Leahy
Examines assessment approaches analytically from different programmatic levels and looks at the implications of these differing approaches. Chapters discuss the implications of cultural differences as well as ideas about knowledge and knowing and the implications these ideas can have for both the participant and the program.
ISBN 0-7879-9840-0

**NEW DIRECTIONS FOR
ADULT AND CONTINUING EDUCATION
IS NOW AVAILABLE ONLINE AT WILEY INTERSCIENCE**

What is Wiley InterScience?

Wiley InterScience is the dynamic online content service from John Wiley & Sons delivering the full text of over 300 leading scientific, technical, medical, and professional journals, plus major reference works, the acclaimed *Current Protocols* laboratory manuals, and even the full text of select Wiley print books online.

What are some special features of Wiley InterScience?

Wiley InterScience Alerts is a service that delivers table of contents via e-mail for any journal available on Wiley InterScience as soon as a new issue is published online.
Early View is Wiley's exclusive service presenting individual articles online as soon as they are ready, even before the release of the compiled print issue. These articles are complete, peer-reviewed, and citable.
CrossRef is the innovative multi-publisher reference linking system enabling readers to move seamlessly from a reference in a journal article to the cited publication, typically located on a different server and published by a different publisher.

How can I access Wiley InterScience?

Visit http://www.interscience.wiley.com

Guest Users can browse Wiley InterScience for unrestricted access to journal Tables of Contents and Article Abstracts, or use the powerful search engine.
Registered Users are provided with a *Personal Home Page* to store and manage customized alerts, searches, and links to favorite journals and articles. Additionally, Registered Users can view free Online Sample Issues and preview selected material from major reference works.
Licensed Customers are entitled to access full-text journal articles in PDF, with select journals also offering full-text HTML.

How do I become an Authorized User?

Authorized Users are individuals authorized by a paying Customer to have access to the journals in Wiley InterScience. For example, a university that subscribes to Wiley journals is considered to be the Customer. Faculty, staff and students authorized by the university to have access to those journals in Wlley InterScience are Authorized Users. Users should contact their Library for information on which Wiley journals they have access to in Wiley InterScience.

ASK YOUR INSTITUTION ABOUT WILEY INTERSCIENCE TODAY!